D1320598

THE NATION'S CHILDREN

in three volumes

THE NATION'S CHILDREN

Edited by Eli Ginzberg

2: DEVELOPMENT AND EDUCATION

Published 1 9 6 0 for the Golden Anniversary
White House Conference on Children and Youth
by COLUMBIA UNIVERSITY PRESS, NEW YORK

GOLDEN ANNIVERSARY
WHITE HOUSE CONFERENCE ON CHILDREN AND YOUTH

HONORARY CHAIRMAN

The President of the United States
Dwight D. Eisenhower

HONORARY VICE CHAIRMAN

The Secretary of Health, Education, and Welfare
Arthur S. Flemming

CHAIRMAN

Mrs. Rollin Brown

VICE CHAIRMEN

Hurst R. Anderson
Philip S. Barba, M.D.
Mrs. James E. Blue
Robert E. Bondy
Erwin D. Canham
Donald K. David
Luther Foster
Msgr. Raymond J. Gallagher

Mrs. Frank Gannett
Edward D. Greenwood, M.D.
Daryl P. Harvey, M.D.
Donald S. Howard
Ruth A. Stout
Rabbi Marc H. Tanenbaum
Rev. Dr. William J. Villaume

SECRETARY

Mrs. Katherine B. Oettinger

ASSOCIATE DIRECTOR

Isabella J. Jones

EXECUTIVE DIRECTOR

Ephraim R. Gomberg

COMMITTEE ON STUDIES

Chairman: Eli Ginzberg *

Leona Baumgartner, M.D.
Mrs. Fitzhugh W. Boggs
Mrs. Wright W. Brooks
Sister Mary de Lourdes *
Jack R. Ewalt, M.D.
Mrs. Otto L. Falk
Mrs. David Graham
Margaret Hickey
Reuben L. Hill, Jr.*
A. John Holden
Rt. Rev. Arthur Carl
    Lichtenberger

Harry M. Lindquist
Mrs. Alvin A. Morrison
Captain Frank J. Popello
William L. Pressly
Milton J. E. Senn, M.D.*
Joseph Stokes, M.D.*
Ruth A. Stout *
Rabbi Marc H. Tanenbaum *
John Tannehill
Ralph W. Tyler *
Whitney M. Young, Jr.*

* Member of the Steering Committee.

CONTENTS

INTRODUCTION

by E L I G I N Z B E R G

NO SOCIETY can afford to be indifferent to the way in which its young people grow up and are educated. For education, in the broadest sense of the term, is the means by which a society transmits, from one generation to the next, the values, knowledge, and skills which alone can insure its survival.

The attitudes a society has toward problems of development and education are as important as—and perhaps even more important than—the institutions that have specific responsibility for developing and educating the young. For many decades, two attitudes have been firmly ensconced in our culture—a belief in the importance of a happy childhood for the development of a sound adult, and a faith in the extension of educational opportunities as a social cure-all.

Each tenet has much to commend it. During this century both Western Europe and the United States have been greatly influenced by dynamic psychology—perhaps even

Eli Ginzberg is Director of the Conservation of Human Resources Project, Director of Staff Studies of the National Manpower Council, and Professor of Economics at Columbia University.

more than by quantum physics. The romantic enthrallment
with the idea of the perfectibility of mankind through the
establishment of a proper social environment has never been
more enthusiastically underwritten than by this country's
conviction that all of its problems can be solved by the
school.

The unending flow of articles and books on child rearing
practices, particularly on the emotional aspects of development, and the ever larger numbers of people who spend
ever longer periods of their lives in school are two indices—
if indices are needed—of the potency of these national convictions.

But science is dynamic and the tempo of the modern
world is not conducive to complacency. Hence, no established belief is long immune from criticism or revision. We
are a pragmatic as well as a romantic people, and when
evidence from the laboratory or from life itself challenges
our beliefs, even our most cherished ones, they will not be
granted immunity. They must stand the test and be proved
or they will be discarded and replaced.

The past several years have witnessed an intensified reap-
praisal of our theories of education in response to a growing
awareness of a discrepancy between the nation's situation at
home and abroad. The gap between the image of ourselves
as we are (or at least as we hope to be) and the reality of
our circumstances present and potential has become increasingly clear, and with increasing clarity has come increasing uneasiness.

"Development and Education," the second volume of

The Nation's Children, presents a series of contributions from three vantage points that are focused on the analysis of the gap between our aspirations and our accomplishments in preparing young people for life: how the gap came to be, what can be done to narrow it, and the extent to which it will probably persist. Each contributor offers his own special knowledge and experience in his discussion of development and education.

Dr. Neel reminds us that important as environment is in human development, heredity sets severe limitations. Only a fraction of the population, certainly less than 10 percent, is inherently capable of making significant contributions to the fields on which our national well-being depends. His analysis further considers the negative impact of heredity: many physical malformations are congenital, and only a few of them are as yet remediable.

Professor Garn, directing his attention to the problems of physical growth and development, makes a series of startling observations: the loss of human life between conception and birth may well be 70 percent; we do not really know why children grow; there is no physiological reason why adolescence should be a period of stress and strain; the only measure of maturity from childhood through adolescence which is truly useful is a hand-wrist x-ray; over-nutrition is a major hazard because, among other reasons, overweight children become overweight adults. While fully aware of the gains which we have made while tinkering with human growth and development, Professor Garn warns us to take stock of the new hazards around us.

In reviewing the state of our knowledge about behavior and personality, Professor Anderson suggests that we consider the growing person as a system—a living organism with a high intake and output of transactions, and with the feedback from the environment playing an important role. Of crucial importance is the child's development of control over his appetites, emotions, and feelings. Professor Anderson states that from a developmental point of view the major aim would be to provide all children with appropriate instruction at appropriate points in time, but in order to do this we need more and better longitudinal studies.

These three essays, rich as they are in information and insight, are even richer in the critique which they provide, both directly and indirectly, of many current dogmas of human development. Their major contribution is to separate the sound from the ephemeral and thereby to lay a firmer basis for schools and other key institutions concerned with development to perform their tasks more effectively.

Dr. Tyler addresses himself directly to the heart of the educational controversy by considering the subject of educational objectives. He reminds us that the very success of the schools has been responsible for much of their present difficulty. The schools today find themselves with so many responsibilities entrusted to them by the American public that they are no longer able to concentrate on their primary task of developing and maintaining the intellectual interests and skills of their students. Dr. Tyler emphasizes the need in a democracy, where the people control the schools, for the public to appreciate the problems that the schools face and the possibilities that exist for the solution of such problems.

In the concluding essay, Dr. Gardner draws attention to the dynamic interplay between public attitudes and educational methods and goals by stressing the fact that Americans will tolerate certain policies directed toward the pursuit of excellence and will reject others. He explains that until the American public clarifies the nature of its commitment to equality there is little prospect of its acting effectively to nurture excellence. Equality does not mean treating all people as if they were exactly alike, but rather providing equality of opportunity for all. Individual differences exist and we must not deny them. Dr. Gardner suggests, however, that even in the face of great differences in ability, including the ability to profit from education, it is not only possible but necessary for the United States to nurture the talents of every citizen—since there are many kinds and levels of excellence —and our dynamic society has need for all of them.

There are four contributions that bear directly on the points of view advanced by Drs. Tyler and Gardner, contributions that help build a bridge from the theoretical to the concrete, from ideology to reality.

In his discussion of the age of science, Professor Zacharias calls attention to our society's increasing need for large numbers of well-trained scientists and suggests that they will emerge because of the strong pressures and incentives that exist to encourage their development. But he goes on to say that the permeation of the whole of contemporary life by science requires that every citizen have some appreciation of its nature and functioning. It is here that the schools face one of their greatest challenges, one that they will be able to meet only if they receive substantial help from the leaders of the scientific community.

In his exploration of the interplay between education and employment, Dr. Wolfbein presents evidence that the age of science has already brought about significant changes in the composition of the labor force, and that the future will see an acceleration of this trend. He quotes a recent advertisement in the Help Wanted section of the New York *Times* through which a large corporation was seeking personnel in eight specialties, but the names of these specialties would not even be recognized by the average college graduate! This is only an extreme example of a general trend in the economy that is resulting in a significant increase in the number and proportion of jobs requiring a high level of training and education. The more the schools can fulfill their basic purpose of training their students to cope with complex intellectual problems, the more they will also be contributing to their students' future occupational adjustment.

During the past two decades the nation's educational structure has undergone two significant extensions through industry and the Armed Services. Mr. Wool gives us an analysis of the extent to which the Armed Services have become a major training institution. Among his major points are these: about 7 out of every 10 men in their middle twenties have had a tour of military duty; the Armed Services today depend on the "soldier-technician"—they have twice as many mechanics as ground combat troops; the Services find it difficult to use men with limited educational background because such men are unable to absorb technical training; during the three years of the Korean conflict, 1.3 million servicemen received training in civilian-type specialties.

Dean Bond, in his analysis of "wasted talent," starts by assuming what Professor Zacharias, Dr. Wolfbein, and Mr. Wool have demonstrated, namely, that ours is a society that requires an increasing number of highly trained persons. It is therefore inefficient as well as inequitable not to encourage the development of young people with high potential. Yet Dean Bond presents some startling evidence of the scale of manpower waste, pointing out that the groups at the upper and lower end of the occupational scale though equal in size produce "talented" children in a ratio of 235 to 1, which reflects primarily the inferior education available to the latter.

Dr. Landis discusses the all-important question of religion and youth and presents a wealth of data about youth membership in church and synagogue as well as attendance figures for different types of religious schools. The figures are large, in fact, impressive. But, as Dr. Landis is quick to point out, those who have delved into the religious commitment of American youth are by no means confident as to what these figures really mean. Undoubtedly religion continues to play a significant role in the lives of large numbers of American youth, but serious questions remain about the extent to which it exercises a fundamental influence on their character formation and behavior.

In their consideration of the child as potential, the Murphys return to a theme that was noted but not elaborated on by several other contributors—that the illumination of the basic issues in educational development is seriously handicapped by the state of our knowledge. The Murphys suggest that the development of potential can best be encouraged by "letting the child choose," for children differ in potential and at different times have different developmental needs. Despite this individual-centered approach, the Murphys not only recognize but stress the reciprocity of the individual and the social world. They end with a plea for national and international unity of human effort without coercion of the individual.

This plea is perhaps only a contemporary translation of the vision of Micah:

Nations shall not lift up sword against nation,
Neither shall they learn war any more.
But they shall sit every man under his vine and his fig tree,
And none shall make them afraid.

THE NATION'S CHILDREN

2: DEVELOPMENT AND EDUCATION

THE GENETIC POTENTIAL

by JAMES V. NEEL, M.D.

AS WE KNOW, each of us represents the outcome
of an interplay between two sets of factors, labeled "heredity" and "environment." In man the interaction between
these factors is generally complicated and sometimes extremely subtle. The present article, devoted to the question
of realizing the genetic potential of our youth, will for
obvious reasons deal primarily with "heredity," with the
knowledge that other contributors to these volumes will
adequately treat the very important "environmental" factors.

The determiners of inherited characteristics are known
as genes. They are, with few exceptions, found in every
cell of the body, physically located in the chromosomes of
the cell nucleus. Genes occur in pairs, one member derived
from the father and one from the mother. There are perhaps 50,000 gene pairs in man. Our present information
suggests that so diverse are the kinds of genes which the
human species possesses that no two individuals, with the

James V. Neel, M.D., is Professor of Human Genetics at the University of Michigan Medical School.

exception of identical twins, are genetically completely alike.

Since a child receives his genetic endowment from his parents, it is only natural that he resemble them in many respects. Since, on the other hand, each child probably represents a unique combination of genes, and since it is not only the kinds of genes present but the combinations in which they occur that determine a child's attributes, each child would from the genetic standpoint be something different from a simple blending of parental characteristics —even if this difference were not already assured by the fact that the environment is never precisely the same for two children.

Because some genes tend to express themselves no matter what the combination in which they occur, i.e., are dominant genes, we often see obvious similarities between a parent and a child. But the genetic redeployment which occurs each generation also permits wide divergences between parents and their offspring. It is possible to demonstrate parent-offspring correlations for a host of traits in a variety of animals, including man. Parents with a superior genetic endowment will tend to transmit this to their offspring. But the process of redeployment referred to above readily permits the birth of defective or inferior children to such superior parents. It also permits the converse: the appearance of superior children from dubious backgrounds.

To the geneticist, the fundamental challenge of a democracy is simple and clear: to permit each child, regardless of background, to realize to the full his innate genetic endowment, mindful always of the rights of others. Much has been achieved in this direction in the United States. Much remains to be done.

The Genetic Extremes

In the United States, existing social and educational facilities are characteristically geared to the average. The individual who falls outside the range for which the system has been developed thus creates a problem for the system. More specifically, while the existing social and educational structure of this country offers as much to the average child as can be found any place in the world today, it may be questioned whether the effort being devoted to the extremes— the exceptionally gifted children and the exceptionally handicapped—is adequate and properly directed.

THE GIFTED. Far more than ever in the past, the present is, and the future will be, characterized by rapid scientific and technological advances. The strength of any country, large or small, lies in its ability to keep abreast or even to lead in these advances.

Not all of us are born with the intellectual endowment which permits us to master higher mathematics, nuclear physics, electronics, advanced chemistry, or certain aspects of economics, sociology, or medicine. The fraction of individuals in our population inherently capable of making the really original contributions in these fields on which our continued national well-being depends is certainly less than

10 percent. It is an inescapable fact that in these rapidly moving days, these individuals constitute our greatest national resource.

In any culture, in any country, at any time, the handicapped, be it for physical or intellectual reasons, tend to come to public attention. Given in this country the added factors of our predominantly Christian and Jewish religious heritage, with its emphasis on compassion, and the American sense of fair play, and there has evolved a system of services for the handicapped in which we may take great pride. None of these services should in any way be weakened. Indeed, many must be strengthened. But it is high time that we faced the proposition that the gifted on whom we unknowingly rely to such an extent deserve from this democracy far more than they have been given in the past. It is high time we faced the fact that by gearing our educational effort to the average, and putting the great bulk of our special efforts into facilities for the handicapped, we have been giving our very able children less than the equal opportunity to which they are entitled.

Concern for the gifted child is by no means unique to the geneticist. However, to the geneticist it has a special significance. To the extent that these special gifts are genetically determined—let us say 50 percent—they tend to be transmitted to the next generation. As has already been brought out, this statement, while correct in a statistical sense, is subject to numerous individual exceptions. Nevertheless, "like begets like." While considerations of this nature may be transgressing the bounds set for this conference, the fact should be borne in mind that our present system not only fails to give the gifted child the same attention in developing his potentialities as the handicapped, but from the standpoint of our species as a whole, places him at an added disadvantage: if he is able to arrange the prolonged training necessary to the full realization of his talents, this often results in deferred marriage and a lower net fertility. To the geneticist this argues strongly for a series of merit scholarships with stipends adequate for marriage at the usual age.

THE HANDICAPPED. Let us turn now to the other end of the spectrum of human variation, to the question of physical and mental handicap. That which is environmentally determined—be it by accidents involving the child during his early years or by accidents during his intra-uterine existence (viral disease of the mother, prolonged lack of oxygen during a difficult delivery)—is essentially preventable. That which is genetic is not so readily preventable.

Genetically determined physical handicap presents a rather different problem from mental handicap. To a growing extent, genetically determined physical handicap is subject to remedial measures. Thus, congenital cataract or harelip, of the genetic type, may be greatly improved by surgical intervention. The outlook in cystic fibrosis of the pancreas, although still leaving a great deal to be desired, is certainly much better now than before the availability of pancreatic extracts and antibiotics.

Moreover, only in its extreme forms is physical handicap a barrier to a rich, useful, and rewarding life. History is replete with individuals who surmounted physical defects, and with our increasingly understanding treatment of such handicaps, the outlook for individuals so afflicted can only improve.

Not so for the mentally handicapped. With the increasing complexity of our social organization, their outlook can only become more perplexing. Children whose limited intellectual endowment would permit them to meet the day to day developments of a simple agrarian community, and even function in a useful capacity, would not be able to so function in New York City.

In considering the problem of the mentally defective individual, it is important from the genetic standpoint to bear in mind constantly certain differences between children with extreme degrees of mental defect (idiots and imbeciles) and those in whom the defect is less pronounced (morons or feebleminded children).[1] By and large, children with an extreme degree of mental defect (idiot or imbecile level) tend to be born of essentially normal parents. The brothers and sisters of such children, if mentally defective, tend to exhibit the same degree of mental defect. On the other hand, children at the moron level tend—on the average—to be born of parents themselves dull. Their siblings, when mentally subnormal, are more often morons than idiots or imbeciles.

These facts may most readily be explained by the following

[1] See J. A. Fraser Roberts, 1952. "The Genetics of Mental Deficiency," *Eugenics Review* (1952), 44:71–83.

assumptions: The extreme degrees of mental defect, when
not due to environmental accidents, are often due to the
fact that the child in question possesses a double dose of
(is homozygous for) a particular recessive gene which has
been carried in hidden form by his parents. Since children
with extreme degrees of mental defect seldom reproduce,
this type of genetically determined defect continues to find
expression each generation only because, in each generation,
normal carriers of the recessive genes by chance marry one
another and unknowingly set the biological stage for the
birth of a child who has received the defective gene from
both his parents. The more moderate degrees of mental
defect, on the other hand, would appear, on the basis of
the evidence just presented plus some too technical to consider here, to be due to the action of multiple genes, both
dominant and recessive. Paradoxically, then, the more extreme types of mental defect tend to have a simpler genetic
etiology.

Now, then, it is an axiom of modern genetics that in the
final analysis most genes exert their influence on the final
form and function of the individual through controlling one
(or more) of the multitude of complex chemical reactions
on which our development and continued functioning depends. Otherwise stated, on the basis of our present knowledge, the ultimate cause of a condition determined by a single
gene will be simpler than of a condition determined by
many genes. It should thus be relatively easier to determine
the precise nature of the basic defect in the more simply

inherited (and severer) types of mental defect than in the more complex (less severe) types. Once the cause of a disease is well understood, the way lies open for its cure.

Extreme Types of Mental Defect

Three examples of our expanding knowledge concerning the cause and cure of the more extreme types of mental defect will suffice to make this point. All of these examples are numerically relatively insignificant, i.e., small numbers of children are involved. But the principle has far-reaching implications.

CRETINISM. This disease is due to a deficiency of thyroid hormone, in consequence of which there is retarded physical and intellectual development. In many parts of the world the most common cause of cretinism is an absence of iodine in the diet, both of mother and child. Since iodine is an essential building block in the synthesis of thyroid hormone, this iodine lack prevents formation of the hormone in normal amounts. With the widespread introduction of iodized salt all over the world, this cause of cretinism is decreasing in importance. However, even after iodized salt becomes freely available in iodine deficient areas, cretinism will not be abolished. Children with cretinism—fortunately few in number—will still be born, not only in iodine deficient areas but elsewhere as well, in whom the cause of the hormone lack is not an exogenous factor, i.e., lack of iodine, but in whom the primary fault is in the thyroid gland itself. In the United States, this latter type of cretinism has always been relatively much more common than the former; indeed, some authorities question whether true iodine-lack cretinism has ever been seen in the United States.

These children in whom cretinism is due to a defect in the thyroid gland itself are of two types. In one group, the thyroid gland appears to be totally absent. These children may in many respects be thought of as children with a congenital malformation. In the second group, the thyroid gland is present, but for genetic reasons unable to function properly. The synthesis of thyroid hormone involves a complicated sequence of chemical reactions. In this latter group, certain of the steps in this sequence are blocked because of genetic deficiencies. These metabolic blocks have now been shown in a number of instances to depend on simple recessive inheritance.

Whether the lack of thyroid hormone is due to the complete absence of a thyroid gland or to the malfunctioning of a genetically defective gland, early recognition of this lack and the administration of adequate amounts of thyroid hormone will prevent the tragedy of cretinism. For the development of the child to be completely normal, recognition of the deficiency and treatment must come during the early months of the child's existence, the earlier the better. If recognition is delayed until, say, one year of age, irreversible damage has usually occurred to the nervous system. Although improvement will result from the initiation of therapy at this age, the child will not, as a rule, completely revert to normal.

Here, then, is an example of a disease, often genetically determined, in which early recognition and adequate treatment will result in a normal development. However, the fundamental defect will remain present throughout life, so that treatment must be continued as long as the individual lives.

PHENYLKETONURIA. This is a type of mental defect, usually severe, first recognized because affected individuals excrete in their urine large amounts of a chemical substance usually present only in trace amounts. The origin of this substance is as follows: The proteins of which our bodies are composed are made up of building blocks termed amino acids. The average protein is a complex substance composed of a thousand or more amino acids. Some of these amino acids can be synthesized by our bodies, but others, known as "essential" amino acids, cannot be so synthesized and we are dependent for normal development on an adequate supply of these latter in the diet. Whenever we take in more amino acids than we need, the body breaks them down into simpler compounds, thereby deriving energy for its various functions. One of the essential amino acids commonly encountered in dietary protein is phenylalanine. Normally, most of the phenylalanine excess to the body's needs is converted into another amino acid, tyrosine, and thence to a series of simpler components. In phenylketonuria, the body is unable to make this conversion, and there accumulate relatively large amounts of other by-products of the breakdown of phenylalanine, by-products which would normally be present only in trace amounts. One of these is phenylpyruvic acid, a phenylketone, which, spilling over into the urine, gives the disease its name. Some of these by-products in large quantities are toxic to the development and functioning of the brain. The inability to make the conversion from phenylalanine to tyrosine seems due to simple recessive inheritance.

In the past several years, there have appeared in the medical literature repeated reports of the results of detecting children with this type of defect at an early age and placing them on a diet very low in phenylalanine. Such a diet must contain enough phenylalanine to meet the body's needs, but still be low enough in this substance to prevent the accumulation of phenylpyruvic acid and related substances. It now appears that the early institution of such a diet may forestall the development of mental defect. The crux of the therapeutic problem is, as in the case of cretinism, early detection. On the basis of the present limited information, it appears that detection at the age of one or two years is too late for maximal benefits: only limited improvement in behavior results, and little or no increase in the I.Q. Since the presence of mental defect is often not suspected before the age of six months, even in a child under close pediatric supervision, the early detection of these children presents a difficult challenge. In this connection, it should be noted that because of the recessive inheritance of this defect it tends to affect multiple children in a family. The group in which careful examination for the presence of this disease is mandatory is composed of the newborn, younger siblings of children in whom the defect has already been diagnosed. Tests of the urine should be carried out as early as possible, but because the telltale phenylpyruvic acid may not appear before three to six weeks of age, a single negative test of the urine at age one month is not sufficient to exclude the disease. Tests of the blood may yield positive results when tests of the urine are negative.

The parents of affected children of course themselves carry in single dose the gene which has such devastating effects when present in double dose in their offspring. It is an interesting and theoretically important fact that frequently, by suitable laboratory tests, these parents can be shown to have defects similar to those in their children, but very much milder in nature, so mild as to cause no symptoms. This observation is theoretically important because it indicates that even so-called recessive genes may have effects when present in single dose. The finding is also important because with further refinements of this test it could become possible to anticipate which marriages were apt to produce defective children. While it would scarcely be practical to apply these tests to all marriages, it would be possible to apply the tests to marriages for which there was a high index of suspicion, such as the marriages of the siblings of a known affected individual. We will return to this possibility later, when we discuss genetic counseling.

GALACTOSEMIA. The principal source of energy in the newborn child is milk sugar, technically known as lactose. Lactose is composed of two simpler sugars, galactose and glucose. In normal digestion, lactose is first broken down into these two constituent sugars and then the galactose is converted to glucose. In galactosemia, the child is unable to change galactose into glucose, a step necessary to the ultimate release of the energy in galactose. The affected child thus literally starves in the midst of plenty. At the same time, the accumulation in the blood and tissues of the galactose which the child cannot utilize appears to have a variety of untoward effects, involving the eyes, the kidney, the liver, and the brain. Mental development may be profoundly retarded. The inability to utilize galactose is inherited as a simple recessive trait.

All of the ill-effects of this inherited defect disappear if the child is placed on a diet free of milk sugar. Again, however, early detection is of the utmost importance, since after two or three months of uncontrolled disease, irreversible changes may have taken place. Fortunately, detection in this case is not so difficult as in the case of phenylketonuria. The affected child is obviously ill shortly after birth, which should bring him to a physician's attention; examination of the urine will reveal the presence of a sugar, which by suitable tests can be shown to be galactose.

Here, too, it is possible to show that the parents of affected children have a minor abnormality, similar to that in the children but not so severe. Thus, the basis of the defect in affected children is the apparent absence of an enzyme whose technical name is P-gal-uridyl-transferase. It has now been shown that in the parents of affected children, this enzyme occurs in approximately half-normal concentration. Because there is a large safety factor in most of the body's functions, even a reduction of as much as 50 percent in the amount of an enzyme may have no obvious ill-effects. The regular reduction in the amount of this enzyme present in the carriers of the defective gene has the same implications for genetic counseling as the defect in phenylketonuria and will be returned to shortly.

Turning now to the problem of borderline mental defect, we do not see the same bright therapeutic possibilities. The prospects of identifying relatively simple and remediable defects are, for reasons stated earlier, less hopeful. For many years to come, the bulk of the effort in this field will probably be directed towards educating the child up to the limits of his capabilities.

Protecting Our Genetic Potential

If, now, it is man's genetic endowment and the culture it has enabled him to create which more than anything else distinguishes man from the other animals which inhabit the earth, it is obviously in the best interests of our species to protect that endowment in so far as possible. Paradoxically, the very type of medical developments discussed in the foregoing pages, which now permit children with serious genetic defects to live normal lives, creates genetic problems for the species, since these children, who would normally not reproduce, now can pass their defective genes on to future generations. The result is inescapably an increase, generation by generation, in the pool of defective genes, with a growing dependence of members of the species on the availability of certain types of medical care. Fortunately, these increases take place at very slow rates indeed; there is no emergency.

In the past, efforts to protect and improve our genetic endowment have gone under the term "eugenics." The eugenics movement has a long and complex background, much of which reflects enthusiasms and strong personal convictions rather than scientific knowledge. Contemporary eugenics has two aspects, a positive and a negative. On the positive side, eugenics is concerned to encourage the reproduction of the fit. While few would quarrel with the thesis that the human species would be well off replacing itself, generation by generation, with its more able and gifted members, practical difficulties at once arise when one attempts to define fitness. We will not essay here the solution of a problem which has eluded so many. However, in the present context we can perhaps agree that a meritorious step in the right direction would be the initiation of measures to obtund, if not relieve completely, the penalty on reproduction now imposed on the poor but able advanced student who must so often defer for a considerable period marriage and a family.

On the negative side, eugenics has been concerned with measures designed to discourage the reproduction of the unfit. Again, problems of definition quickly arise. While there are some few genetic unfortunates whose combination of undesirable inherited traits is such that the world would undoubtedly be better off were these not passed on to the next generation, one quickly moves from a relatively few clear decisions to a great many ambiguous situations. It has been the position of the author that so little do we understand of the forces that have shaped the human species, so limited is our knowledge of human genetics, that organized attempts to influence the reproductive behavior of segments of the human race are for the present most unwise. In passing, attention should be called to the genetically indefensible nature of the so-called eugenic laws of many of our states.

Genetic Counseling

But while organized attempts to influence groups of individuals in their reproductive behavior appear unwise, the fact remains that family planning is an established aspect of our reproductive pattern, and one element in planning is the probable nature of the children. Many families into which there have been born one or more children with genetically determined disease are deeply concerned over the likelihood of subsequent recurrences. The reproductive patterns of such families will often be influenced by their understanding of this likelihood. Recent years have seen the development over the country of clinics devoted to attempting to explain real or fancied genetic situations to concerned parents. The genetic counseling of such clinics is an accepted facet of modern medical practice.

Genetic counseling embraces a variety of activities. The most common type of problem with which heredity clinics have to deal is the probability of recurrence of a particular disease or defect, once an affected child has appeared in a family. A somewhat different type of problem arises when prospective marital partners, conscious of a genetic problem in the family background, request advice concerning the genetic risks for their children. As has already been brought out, there are available an increasing number of laboratory tests useful in the detection of the carriers of inherited disease, which can assist in meeting the particular problems of such individuals. The advisability of cousin marriage is a perennial problem at heredity clinics. Finally, some clinics have the resources to deal with problems of paternity exclusion and racial ancestry, especially in relation to adoption.

It is a social paradox that often it is the parents with the most to offer children, both from the standpoint of genetics and sociology, who are most concerned about the possibility of abnormality in their offspring. It is part of the responsibility of the individual engaged in genetic counseling to lead parents to a rounded and balanced picture of both their positive and negative potential contributions to a child.

Avoidance of Agents Producing Mutations

There exist at the present time widely divergent viewpoints concerning many aspects of eugenics. But concerning a related topic, which also involves the genetic well-being of future generations, there is a remarkable unanimity of opinion. Geneticists in general agree that the human species should certainly avoid exposure to noxious agents likely to harm our genetic endowment. This brings us to a consideration of attitudes towards ionizing radiation and other agents capable of bringing about inherited changes in the properties of the genes, changes termed mutations.

The demonstration that x-rays and related types of ionizing radiation could produce mutations in exposed animals goes back only a little over thirty years. Concern over the possible genetic consequences of our exposure to increasing amounts of ionizing radiation stems from the following considerations: A certain number of "spontaneous" mutations occur in our

germ cells and are transmitted to our offspring each generation. The ultimate causes of these mutations are poorly understood. The majority of mutations appear to have undesirable effects. In a state of nature, natural selection would
tend to eliminate the undesirable mutations and conserve
those advantageous to the species. For each animal species,
including our own, there is thought to be an optimum mutation rate. If the mutation rate is too low, then the species
will not have a sufficient store of variability to draw on in
meeting changing conditions, and the species is in danger of
being left behind in the competitions of life, especially if
the environment changes radically (as seems to be the case for
man today). On the other hand, if mutation rates are too
high, then the rate of introduction of new mutations into
our germ plasm may exceed the rate with which the undesirable majority of mutations can be eliminated. While,
because of improved socioeconomic circumstances and ad-
vancing levels of medical care, the species can undoubtedly
tolerate some increase in mutation rates, there must be a
limit. X-rays, which produce mutations very like those oc-
curring spontaneously, create a problem because they threaten
to upset the natural balance between the occurrence of
spontaneous mutations and natural selection.

The unit of measurement of x-ray dose is the *roentgen*
or *r* unit. The early genetic work with x-rays involved relatively large doses of radiation, of the order of 1,000 or more
r. More recent work has involved much lower doses, some as
low as 25 or 50 *r*. Over this entire dose range, the number of
mutations produced by a given treatment has been propor-

tional to the amount of radiation delivered to the germ cells. Although thus far, because of their extremely laborious nature, experiments have not been carried out at very low dose levels, say 5 or 10 r, it would seem to be on the side of caution to assume that even at these low doses x-rays will produce mutations.

Much of the experimental work has involved the delivery of the radiation dose to the germ cells over a very short time interval. Recent investigations suggest that if a given dose of radiation is spread out over a considerable period of time, it may have a lesser effect than if all were delivered within a few minutes. This is an observation of considerable practical importance, since most human exposures involve repeated, very small doses rather than a single or several large doses. Again, in facing the unknown, it seems best to proceed cautiously and assume that no matter how low-level and protracted the radiation exposure, genetic effects will ensue.

What, now, are the facts of radiation exposure in the twentieth century? A study in 1957 sponsored by the Committee on Radiation Genetics of the National Academy of Sciences brought out a number of interesting points. To the geneticist, the important radiation is that delivered to the germ cells. The study showed that in the United States, by the time the average citizen reaches the age of thirty, he or she has received from natural sources a total (cumulative) dose to the germ cells of approximately 3 r. This dose results from the natural radioactivity of the atmosphere, the earth, and the body itself. From man-made sources, the average individual receives another 4.5 r. The bulk of this radiation

comes from the medical uses of x-rays. A small fraction—
perhaps .1 to .2 r will result from fall-out due to the testing of atomic weapons, assuming testing continues at more
or less the same rate as during 1951–1955, and current estimates concerning the rate with which atmospheric con-
tamination is deposited are essentially correct.

At these low levels of radiation, and with the many uncon-
trollable variables in human populations, it almost certainly
will be impossible to demonstrate genetic effects from these
additional, man-made exposures to radiation. Even in the
children born to the survivors of the atomic bombings of
Hiroshima and Nagasaki, where the radiation doses were far
greater, it was only with great difficulty that a small effect
on the sex ratio could be demonstrated, while no effect on
the frequency of congenital malformations was seen. Nevertheless, it seems an inescapable conclusion that some additional mutations will result from these increased exposures.
It follows from this that efforts to minimize our exposure
to radiation are in order.

To what lengths one should go to minimize radiation exposures is one of the hotly debated topics among scientists today.
The decisions to be made involve striking difficult balances
between gain and loss. With respect to medical exposure, the
gain is relatively easy to visualize. It is difficult to conceive
of the practice of modern medicine without recourse to x-rays,
and no responsible student of the problem has yet suggested
any curtailment of procedures for which there are sound
medical indications. On the other hand, there are sometimes

elective procedures involving the use of x-rays, with respect to which increasing medical caution will undoubtedly be apparent in the future.

In passing, the point should be made that technical improvements in radiology promise to reduce to perhaps one-half the amount of radiation delivered by a variety of standard x-ray practices. Many of these improvements, which involve both the machines and the types of film they employ, are already being put into effect—some are still in the developmental stage.

Also in passing, attention should be directed towards the importance of the public's attitude towards x-ray exposure in determining our cumulative dose. One concrete example will suffice. Recent years have witnessed an increasingly critical attitude of the general public towards the medical profession, an attitude reflected in the growing frequency of malpractice suits. Now, of 1,000 persons who consult a physician because of an apparently minor accident, there may be one or two who have a cracked or chipped bone, a type of injury not so obvious as the usual break. Many such fractures may be suspected on the basis of a persistence of soreness beyond the usual time, i.e., they would be recognized and treated properly a relatively few days after the accident, with the patient none the worse for the delay. Unfortunately, the physician who delays taking an immediate x-ray runs the risk of a malpractice suit in the very rare case in which an unsuspected fracture is found later. These circumstances foster the unnecessary use of x-rays.

The problem of gain and loss is more complex when we turn to the consequences of nuclear weapons testing. Doubtless, every responsible citizen would welcome an end to continued testing, a testing which is, after all, only a symptom of a much more basic problem, East-West tensions. But until satisfactory agreements can be reached, the alternative to continued testing would seem to be unilateral action which might not only jeopardize our position and that of our allies, but also open the way to a far greater loss of life than will ever result from the testing program.

Thus far in this aspect of the discussion, we have referred to x-rays as if they were the only agent capable of accelerating mutation rates to which the human species was exposed. The fact is that the same expanding and wonderful medical armamentarium which provides the physician with effective approaches to so many diseases contains numerous agents known to influence mutation rates in experimental organisms. The mutations produced by these agents are quite similar to those produced by x-rays. A partial list of these drugs includes ether, chloral hydrate, codeine, benzedrine, cortisone, urethane, colchicine, peroxides, and chelating agents. Even caffein has been found to be a weak producer of mutations in the fruit fly, that favorite subject of the experimental geneticist. As in the case of x-rays, the use of these drugs certainly creates no acute genetic problems. But the genetic potentialities involved must be mentioned if we are to have an overall approach to the problems created by man's increasing mastery over self and environment.

Conclusion

Only in relatively recent years have we come to some realization of the full complexity of our genetic heritage, and the complicated and subtle fashion in which its expression is shaped by environmental factors. The present century in retrospect may well be characterized as the century in which man assumed responsibility for creating his own environment. From fleeing storm and pestilence, dreading droughts and crop failures, man has emerged possessed of what as recently as a few hundred years ago would have seemed almost supernatural control over the world about him. With this new control over environment comes awesome responsibilities, and to the geneticist the greatest of all these is the creation of the circumstances in which human evolution may continue and the genetic potentiality of each individual be realized to the fullest extent possible.

GROWTH AND DEVELOPMENT

by STANLEY M. GARN

FROM the moment of conception and for more than twenty years the human organism both grows and develops. Shortly after fertilization, when one venturesome sperm successfully penetrates an ovum, there is an increase in the number of cells; that is *growth*, and growth continues well into the third decade. By the time the number of divided cells in the cell-mass reaches sixteen or so, *development* (differential growth) truly begins. Development continues throughout the growing period, and is heightened at the time of sexual maturity.

However many ages William Shakespeare penned for man, there are five distinct stages of growth and development. Each of these stages is unique, self-limiting, and has its own problems both practical and investigative. No one scientist is equipped intellectually or instrumentally to study them all. Few individuals not concerned with growth research are aware of all of the complications. The practical

Stanley M. Garn is Chairman of the Physical Growth Department of the Fels Research Institute and Associate Professor of Anthropology at Antioch College.

problems of one stage of development often refer back to investigative problems at an earlier stage.

Consider the first trimester, the first three months of gestation, the period during which the embryo comes to look obviously and unquestionably human. This is a period of enormous wastage: at least 3 out of every 10 known conceptions never get beyond the first trimester. Since very early embryonic losses commonly go unnoticed, the true wastage before birth may well be 70 percent of all conceptions! The first trimester, moreover, is a time of tremendous danger to the embryo: though tiny, its rapidly developing cells are highly susceptible to oxygen-deprivation, toxins, and viral agents. It is during the first trimester that almost all developmental defects—the cleft palates, missing limbs, blindnesses, and monstrosities—we see at birth occur. Possibly a single virus affecting susceptible tissue at a critical horizon results in the association between Mongolism and leukemia. The one bright side of the picture of embryonic wastage and prenatal loss is that the grossest of the defects and the most lethal of the genes never get beyond the first trimester. Thus we are spared untoward numbers of defective individuals and our genetic makeup constantly purifies itself by prenatal attrition.

From the sixth through the ninth month of pregnancy, hazards are fewer and the completion of major stages of development makes the fetus less vulnerable to injury. Yet it is in this time period when neural growth may be set back by environmental insults too mild to yield gross anatomical defects. Nutritional deficiencies during later pregnancy may lead to unsound teeth, jaw-face defects, and disturbances of behavior and personality observable in later life. Extreme prematurity, one of the hazards we have not yet learned to cope with successfully, may in part represent veritable rejects from the maternal womb. Many problems of growth and development during later pregnancy remain to be solved including the causes of physiologic "giantism" of diabetic progeny. As we save the majority of adult diabetics, and carry more and more of them successfully through pregnancy, we see with increasing frequency the peculiar explosive growth of many of their progeny.

Growth during infancy and growth during childhood are facts of life we all know something about. Although we know that children grow, we do not really know why they grow. We do not fully understand the implications of fatness (fat infants do not grow faster, but fat children do). We know a tremendous amount about bone growth, yet we do not know the exact sites of action of many of the hormones and enzymes we have isolated. We know next to nothing about the growth and development of the teeth, indeed, the commonly quoted standards for tooth formation are based on only 25 infant cadavers! While we can measure size and calculate the rate of growth, and compare both to norms, the protein requirements of infants are still to be worked out.

The child moves toward maturity with the secretion of several pituitary hormones that stimulate the gonads to secrete steroid hormones that build muscle, that accelerate and then terminate bone growth, and that bring about the production of mature germ cells. Some of the obvious changes during puberty we all know. In the male, less commonly in the female, there is a period of accelerated growth, sometimes exceeding four inches a year, when the cuffs of the pants shoot upward from the shoelaces to above the ankles, and great quantities of foodstuffs move through the alimentary canal.

Traditionally, in our culture, adolescence is a period of stress and strain but there is no physiological reason for it. Twenty milligrams of testosterone is not unsettling except to a few dozen sebaceous glands. "Adolescent rebellion" occurs in the hypogonadal lad as well as in the normal boy. Growth, itself, does not result in awkwardness. Despite a raft of elementary textbooks, an overnight increase of two-hundredths of an inch hardly unsettles the balance of Joe, or Pete, or Tom, or Dick. We cannot blame undesirable adolescent behavior on growth, genes, or glands, but only on a culture that has no meaningful place for the adolescent. This however, does not lessen the vicissitudes of adolescent growth and its effect on the adult-to-be. The fat adolescent is unhappy in a lean milieu. Six chances out of ten she or he will eat a broad path directly into fat adulthood. At the other end of the plate, fad diets and self-directed starvation lead to nutritional deficiencies. In our mammocentric culture the bosomy lass may enjoy temporary popularity at the expense of her lithe-figured peers. In the sports-oriented school the lean or nonmuscular boy may gravitate into an intellectual corner, or into a mischievous group. Lacking muscular outlets the muscular lad is more likely to find prestige in an antisocial gang. Differences in growth rate, physique, and fat-patterning may have tremendous repercussions on the adolescents themselves. Yet we "democratically" believe in one school, one curriculum, and one set of social expectations for a variety of growing human organisms of different shapes and sizes.

Sooner or later growth-cessation is reached, that is "young adulthood," and "early maturity." At this time growth is no longer easily measured en masse, and development becomes more subtle to detect. By fifteen or so the majority of girls are prospective mothers and by seventeen almost all boys can become fathers. Except in the lowest social groups we try to forestall both possibilities with monastic institutions and by ritualized group activities. For military purposes an eighteen-year-old is an adult, regardless of the extent of epiphyseal union, yet we now know that muscle mass increases through the twenties. Stature can increase at least through age twenty-five. Some of the more sex-specific characteristics continue to develop even after the irrevocable declines in performance have made their appearance. The period of growth, the period of maturity, and the period of aging are not discrete. Aging begins in some tissues long before growth is completed in others. From conception on, the rate of cell-growth declines and by the time measurable growth is completed, the human organism already shows demonstrable decreases in performance.

Physical growth is an inseparable part of physical aging. Research on growth, while directed primarily at the "growing" period, has obvious bearings on gerontological research and the whole problem of decreased physical performance in the later years.

The Adequacy of Growth

Quite often a major aim of growth research is to provide norms, standards, charts, and techniques for appraising the adequacy of growth. In many nations where science must be immediately "useful" to command funds, this is too frequently the only task allowed to growth research. Even here, where the pure research of today becomes the applied science of tomorrow, growth research is often construed simply as a search for yardsticks. In a nation dedicated to its children, sincerely interested in offering them every material and psychological advantage, such an attitude is understandable. Who of us does not wish for our children the opportunities for optimum growth? Yet what is "optimum" growth? Poor growth is commonly associated with small size. This is true in under-nutrition, in protein-deficiency states, in vitamin deficiencies, and as the result of a variety of emotional disturbances. Size, moreover, is easily measured, and can be compared to tables of averages and percentiles for boys and girls of various ages from birth through statural maturity. The big question is *which* table of averages and percentiles?

Children have been getting bigger. The Bowditch tables of a hundred years ago are now historical mementoes. The Baldwin-Wood tables, once the model of their kind, are now hopelessly obsolete (though still furnished gratis by enterprising manufacturers). While up-to-date tables of size-for-

age are obviously necessary, and continuing revision of such
data justified, there is a tarnished cloud on the silver lining.
Since today's norms will be obsolete a decade hence, since
they will be uniformly too small like last-year's jeans, is
average size-for-age really an indication of the adequacy of
growth of a particular child?

As is commonly known, there is a fair relationship between family wealth and children's size. This relationship
is a complicated one beginning in prenatal life, and is not
just a matter of calories consumed or vitamin pills eaten.
On the average, doctors, lawyers, and managers are taller and
they have taller children: day-laborers, itinerant workers, and
migratory laborers have smaller offspring. Here in America
the socio-economic span in children's stature is far less than
in Eastern and Middle-Eastern countries. Still, it poses a particular problem—that of which norms to use. In the Middle
East this relationship between size and wealth holds potential political dynamite. In our own country, is the "optimum" average the national average, the collegiate average,
the lower-class average, or what? If we are to set down
norms for Americans, norms to use in growth appraisal, what
norms and whose norms ought we to use? Should we use the
larger Los Angeles norms, the smaller Boston norms, or
compromise on Iowa norms? For the Puerto Rican children
in New York, and for other recent immigrants or genetically
distinct groups, what are the appropriate norms to employ?

Stature, that is length or height, has the dual advantage of
being easily taken, and of being relatively simple to com-
prehend. However, problems arise with long-legged popu-

lations, such as many American colored groups, or with the short-legged Eskimo and Aleut: for such groups "tallness" or "shortness" must be separately interpreted. Weight, moreover, is an excessively complicated measure, and therefore any attempt to utilize weight or to relate weight to height brings in unforeseen variables. As we know now some of the young men rejected from the draft as being "overweight" were actually less fat than the average. They had exceptionally high fat-free weights. There are fat "underweight" children and lean "overweight" children. Without such additional measures as fat-folds, or radiographic measurements of outer fat, the very information we want from weight is too easily lost in the numbers. Overweight or underweight are realistic measures of fatness only at the extremes. In between there is no substitute for measuring fat itself.

One further variable must be added to this section on growth appraisal, and that is maturity status. Neither height nor weight nor amount of stored fat can be adequately interpreted until maturity status is taken into account. At 39 inches tall Johnny may be hopelessly behind in maturity, and Willy surprisingly ahead. At present, the only measure of maturity truly useful from childhood through adolescence is a hand-wrist x-ray. Properly taken the gonadal exposure from such an x-ray is under 0.001 mr, equivalent to a few minutes natural background radiation, that is the amount absorbed in a few minutes of normal living! The information from such a radiograph is not equalled by any other measure we know of now.

It is possible to say that a child is tall or short, in reference to reasonably appropriate norms. It is also possible to say whether the child is fat or lean, or average, below average or above average in maturity status. The meaning of all of this, however, is quite unknown except at the extremes where the clinician must take charge. Without question, growth can be speeded by stuffing the child, and growth can be slowed by withholding food. Periods of exceptionally slow growth are suspect but beyond this can we actually appraise the adequacy of growth?

With the techniques now at hand, and using the well-to-do as a baseline or reference, it is indeed possible to make growth appraisals in individual children or in populations where growth adequacy is a problem. But for the bulk of American childhood, for the children of tall parents or the taller children of short parents, neat and precise growth appraisals (using charts and graphs) are less effective than the nonmetrical but skilled appraisal of a pediatrician or family doctor who knows both the child and his parents.

The major growth studies of America, at Berkeley, at Denver, at the Fels Research Institute, and at Harvard, and the newer programs in Philadelphia and now Louisville, have accumulated and are accumulating irreplaceable, detailed lifetime growth curves of several thousand children. Numerous patterns of growth can be documented in each of these series. By careful analysis and painstaking reference to the health histories and to the dietary records, these analyses will help us to know just how much growth-appraising we reasonably can do. Until then the evaluation of growth adequacy by measurement, by chart, and by graph remains macroscopic. We can pick out the small child, the thin child, the late-maturing child, and the child who simply fails to grow. The meaning and practical importance of the minor deviations, the statistically atypical growth patterns of apparently still-normal children—these we still have to discover. To succeed, more than a yardstick and a weighing-scale will have to be used, and no copyrighted way of putting height and weight together will make up for the limitations of these two useful, traditional, but still limited measures.

The Problem of Overnutrition

The White House Conference in 1930 coincided with the great depression. The major concern then was with inadequate nutrition. Millions of American children were on short rations both calorie-wise and nutrient-wise. Moreover, as their parents economized on coal, and their clothing became threadbare and thin, caloric expenditures of the body were viciously raised while caloric intake unfortunately diminished.

Today the situation is vastly different. Caloric intake is at an all-time high. Vitamin supplementation is inevitable and unavoidable, even in candy bars and all-day suckers. Homes are hotter, clothing is warm though light. Moreover, many old avenues for caloric expenditure are closed. Two pervasive problems of our decade, obesity and parking, involve the children even more than the adult population. To many pediatricians, overnutrition is a singular concern, and the symposium on overnutrition at the Ninth International

Congress of Pediatrics at Montreal in 1959 was packed to standing room.

Exactly what are the effects of overnutrition? Some we know. The fatter the child is, the faster he grows, the earlier he matures, and the sooner he achieves final stature. The fat child, therefore, particularly the fat girl, not only has the temporal disadvantage of being fat (with all of its psychological sequels) but the further disadvantage of being sexually mature in a peer-group of the sexually immature.

Fatness in childhood, moreover, is of more than transitory importance. A recent study has shown that 80 percent of overweight children in one community became overweight adults. A pattern possibly leading to cardio-vascular and renal diseases, and a reduced life expectancy, was thus traceable back to the formative years. Individuals who were fat in childhood are less susceptible to caloric control as adults. And, today, an increasing proportion of our juvenile population appears to be becoming fat. We should no longer exhibit American height-weight data with unalloyed pride, and we need not compliment ourselves on the earlier age of sexual maturity. This latter accomplishment is beginning to concern some of our school boards, who see a physiological reason for realigning the eighth grade with the high school, and diminishing the length of the junior-high school period.

The reasons for increasing fatness are at least partly comprehensible. The availability of food is one obvious cause. Food supplements, largely sugars, are being doled out to the children by their parents. Chocolate milk-amplifiers under any name are largely flavored corn syrup. Through the stimulation of advertising, tap water is being replaced by sugared juices, milk, and carbonated drinks. Snacks have become a ritualized part of the movies and are inseparably associated with television viewing. Avenues for caloric expenditure are gradually diminishing. In many of our great cities, safe opportunities for strenuous play now scarcely exist. There is room at the curb for father to lather the automobile, but precious little space for tag. As suburbia expands into the denuded suburbs, there are fewer trees to climb, fewer things to do. The car-pool and the school-bus reduce the energy expenditure and the ranch house no longer provides calorie-expending stairs to climb.

These strictures would be strictly academic, if the picture was only of rosy-cheeked and chubby cherubs, but there are dark clouds considerably bigger than a man's body. The general hazards of obesity in adulthood we already know. From mortality data "optimum" weight is already well below "average" weight. Moreover, there is increasing evidence that atherosclerosis, far from being an exclusively adult predisposition, actually begins in childhood. Does earlier maturity lead to earlier demise? Are we eating our way to the cemetery beginning in the perambulator?

Moreover, the American child's diet, once characterized as one big milkshake, comes perilously close to a dietary known to be atherogenic. If 35 percent of his calories come from fats, is junior being prepared starting in nursery school for a coronary occlusion? Reviewing the dietaries of some of our teen-agers, I am struck by the resemblance to the diet that Dr. Olaf Mickelsen uses to create obesity in rats. Frappes, fat-meat hamburgers, bacon-and-mayonnaise sandwiches, followed by ice cream may be good for the farmer, good for the undertaker, and bad for the populace.

Admittedly, we are at a crossroads. From an undernourished past we have succeeded in providing a dietary and a way of life for near-maximum growth. In so doing we may have passed the point of maximum health returns. Can we create a cultural climate in which calories are reduced? Can we make popular the kind of low-fat diet that Irvin Page is developing? And, in fact, is it not our purpose to see beyond childhood? Should we not keep the six-year-old from eating his way into a premature grave at sixty even if it means making life less joyous in the childhood period? Again is it our purpose to emulate Banta's starved water-fleas, and McCance's undernourished rats? They lived longer, but is longevity the primary aim?

Newer Hazards to Growth and Development

In the past forty years much has been accomplished to reduce prenatal wastage, to decrease the proportion of the prematurely born, to pull feeble infants through the hazardous first weeks, and to promote sound bone growth during infancy and childhood. Hormonal therapy and bed rest are both employed in the event of threatened abortion, and a variety of approaches are now used to prevent later but still precipitous entrance into the world. The smallest of the "premies" are boxed, warmed, humidified, and oxygenated. Children of all ages are liberally vitaminized with a well-advertised hand.

Many of the results have been heart-warming indeed. The mortality of the larger "premies" has been so much reduced that the birth of a four-pound or even a three-pound infant is no longer a calamity. Since the days of cod-liver oil, D-deficiency rickets has practically disappeared. However, reduced prenatal human wastage, the disappearance of many vitamin deficiencies, and sound bone growth have not been achieved without certain new hazards. Some of these hazards are currently a real source of concern.

In the event of threatened abortion, certain steroid hormones, namely progesterone and progesterone-like substances are used. Such substances may be routinely prescribed for women with a history of abortion. Related steroids have also been utilized in later pregnancy. There is now mounting evidence that in some proportion of cases, partial sex reversal does result from hormonal therapy. Girl babies have become masculinized *in utero* and some boy babies have become feminized. The whole course of normal postnatal physical and emotional growth has thus been altered by prenatal treatment. The small proportion of cases of sex reversals that occur may be a small danger in comparison to the number of pregnancies that would otherwise have terminated prematurely. But here is one example of a modern measure that returns some portion of evil in return for demonstrable good.

As a result of improved clinical care, including much more prenatal attention, it is now safe for the older woman to bear children. If otherwise healthy, she faces scarcely more danger than a twenty-year-old. Yet no medical care has yet been able to minimize the chances of her bearing a

Mongolian imbecile. With mounting age the probability of
Mongoloid offspring markedly increases. In this year of cele-
bration for Charles Darwin, it is pertinent to remember
that Emma Wedgwood Darwin was delivered of a Mongolian imbecile in her fiftieth year. Making it safe to have
children later increases the probability of Mongolism. Again
we must learn to calculate the risks.

Many authorities are beginning to cast a jaundiced eye at
elaborate attempts to retain conceptuses that threaten to
abort. They point to the much higher incidence of abnormalities in the early adventurers right up to the seventh and
eighth months. A very high proportion of the very prematurely born exhibit malformations. The smaller of the
still-viable premies commonly exhibit symptoms of neural
damage: evidently their prematurity stems from multiple
developmental problems. At what cost does the increased
probability of defective development outweigh the desira-
bility of saving the infant? In this instance is there a special
danger of telling nature she does not know her own business?

As an example of the influence of technology on normal
growth and development, let us consider the incubator.
Long used for chickens, the incubator came to be employed
for the human infant just about forty years ago. As time
progressed, simple boxes heated with hot water bottles became more complex, more automatic, and more efficient.
It was possible to provide a high oxygen atmosphere in
tightly sealed isolettes and this, as we now know, too often
resulted in *retrolental fibroplasia*, a developing blindness resulting from overly high oxygen levels at a critical period

in the smallest of the prematures. Obviously, technology outstripped knowledge of developmental anatomy. We are paying now in special schools, and special programs for children who had retrolental fibroplasia a decade and more ago for yet another hazard to normal growth development.

When one thinks of vitamins one does not ordinarily think of possible dangers. In most cases dangerous doses of vitamins are far in excess of the physiological (i.e., useful) dosage. Yet hypervitaminosis-D and hypervitaminosis-A are recurring concerns. Marked abnormalities in bone formation and in growth occur in infants who eat large amounts of fortified butter or oleomargerine a day and in children who are overly indulged by parents engaged in their own private practice of pseudo-medicine. This is not a transient danger, moreover, for some of the self-styled food authorities and prophets of Health-Through-Eating consider vitamins to be cold remedies, intelligence improvers, and food substitutes. With parents who leave insecticides, carbon tetrachloride, arsenic, or strychnine about, health education is a good remedy, but it may also have dangers. Hypervitaminosis, even though resulting from good intentions, is probably an increasing hazard to normal growth and development.

In the past, most of the hazards faced by the child led to retarded growth and delayed development. Today, the availability of synthetic and natural hormones poses a real threat, one frequently resulting in abnormally accelerated sexual development. Children have got hold of stilbesterol intended for animal feeding. They have swallowed their mother's bust-improving pills; they have greased themselves with estrogenic creams. Since sex hormones are increasingly used in the veterinarian's management of pet disorders, the opportunities of eating Fido's pills and kitty's capsules abound. There are reports in the veterinary literature of premature sexual development resulting from ingestion of such substances. The common tendency to use steroid-thyroid "cocktails" in the management of the aged pet pose a further threat. While foods containing residual amounts of stilbesterol do not pose hazards for children, the average home increasingly holds dangers and the possibility of abnormally accelerated development.

While the appearance of antibiotic-resistant strains of bacteria and secondary manifestations of antibiotic sensitivity in children are outside of the scope of this essay, the question of continued antibiotic therapy must be considered in relation to growth development. Pigs, geese, sheep, and cattle grow bigger on antibiotic-supplemented feed. It is questionable however, whether such supplementation is appropriate to the human child. While aureomycin has been used with alleged success in "improving" the growth of children with certain bone disorders, the overall value of such a program remains doubtful. We know that the growth of hogs is improved if tranquilizers are added to their diet, pigs being more skittish and erratic eaters than their reputation has led us to believe. Yet this success at the animal level does not make it safe to use tranquilizers routinely in improving the dietary practices of finicky eaters among our boys and girls.

X-radiation is a much talked about hazard with too little

distinction made between a 1000 roentgen local therapeutic dose, a 500 roentgen total-body lethal dose, a 0.1 roentgen localized diagnostic dose or the 0.001 milliroentgen (0.00001 roentgen) gonadal dose from a properly shielded diagnostic radiograph. The normal *daily* background radiation is large in comparison to the gonadal radiation for many properly taken diagnostic x-rays.

Nevertheless, dental x-rays often repeated in children constitute a present area of concern, not so much from the standpoint of gonadal dosages but in view of the rather large total dosages that can accrue from a number of series of full-mouth radiograms. While cumulative small dosages apparently have less biological effect than single large doses of the same order of magnitude, the effect of 100 roentgens or more of x-radiation to the developing teeth and jaws is of current concern.

At the same time, the advantages of careful dental radiography are considerable and should not be neglected. One cannot ask a pedodontist to exert every possible skill in treating a child's teeth without affording the dentist the opportunity to make whatever diagnostic x-rays necessary. Here is one area where technological advances in radiography have fallen well behind. Even with present techniques, it is possible to obtain adequate radiographs of the posterior teeth with a much lower total dosage of x-radiation. But the films, which have been speeded up by 100 percent in the last three years, need to be ten times faster before repeated full-mouth x-rays cease to be a source of immediate concern.

Progress in any area of human achievement consists of

many steps forward and a few steps back. Progress can be measured in terms of the proportion of the newborn that live to maturity. As compared to groups where 2 out of 3 children never reach maturity, the extent of progress in our own country is notable indeed. Our ability to minimize prenatal and neonatal wastage is considerable. It is improving and will improve still further. Yet we must be aware that each step of progress holds with it the possibility of inherent danger, that some proportion of the children saved will ultimately be lost because of the measures used to save them. Moreover, some proportion of the children so saved, though not lost, will be blind or deaf; they will grow abnormally or they will attain sexual development prematurely or even in the wrong direction.

We are now at the point where we can tinker with human growth and development from the very moment of conception right on to early maturity. It would be folly to decry progress or to demand a return to the cruder days when a newborn infant had less than a 50-50 chance of living for one year, and where the probabilities of his growing adequately and well were far smaller than that. We need not be pessimistic. Nevertheless we are building up hazards, and it is an appropriate time to take stock of the hazards that exist.

THE DEVELOPMENT OF BEHAVIOR
AND PERSONALITY

by J O H N E . A N D E R S O N

THE MOST obvious fact of growth and development is progress from infancy to adult life. All of us have known infants and adults. So common and universal are growth and development that we take them for granted without realizing how complex and wonderful they are.

The baby is already nine months along the course of development when he is born. He moves through infancy into childhood; then after puberty, into adolescence. After growth ceases he, as an adult, has a long period of maturity with full power, after which come the declines of senescence. Death ends the life cycle. All living beings go through this course, unless it is terminated prematurely by disease or accident. Children cannot be kept as babies; nor can adolescents be treated as children. With growth children and adolescents assert their independence and take their places in life as adults.

Growth and development are not merely changes in phys-

John E. Anderson is Director of the Institute of Child Development and Welfare and Professor of Psychology at the University of Minnesota.

ical size or bodily proportions. Changes occur in almost
every relation within and without the human being. For
our present purposes, we may call attention to the increased
range of objects and experiences to which the growing person responds; to his increased strength, speed and motor
skill; to his growing intellectual and problem solving capacity; to his greater ease in using language and communicating
with others; to his enriched social life with its web of interrelations; and to his changing interests, activities, and values.
From the dependence of infancy the person moves to the
maturity and responsibility of adult life.

What Is a Child?

Before describing growth and development, we ask in very
general terms, what is a child? He is, first, a complex physical
chemical system for converting food into energy; and second,
a system of sense organs, nerves, and muscles which, by
responding to stimulation, directs energy into the channels
we know as behavior or action. Thus there are two aspects
of life.

The first aspect is that of impulse, drive, emotion, and
feeling. It furnishes the impulsion or motivation which,
through the operations of the nervous system, makes adjustment possible. In the world of impulse, the person seeks to
meet biological needs. He takes in food, eliminates waste,
breathes in air, reproduces his kind. These are the appetites
which make existence and reproduction possible. Next come
the emergency reactions, which under appropriate condi-

tions move the person to anger, to fear, or to exciting love. These exciting emotions mobilize resources for short periods, heighten the energy output, and produce the more varied, more intense, and more rapid behavior which makes it possible to meet an emergency. Then there are the attachments or likes and dislikes. These attitudes toward objects, persons, and relations affect all aspects of behavior.

Throughout infancy, childhood, and adolescence we can follow the modification of appetite, emotion, and feeling. Much of development centers in the building of controls and the direction of energy into activities that are personally and socially useful. As a result, in the older child we find learned ways of persisting in particular activities until a goal is reached. Tensions organize energy output to achieve various purposes.

The controls which appear, however, are in large part a function of the second aspect of the person. This aspect is concerned with sensing and perceiving objects, persons, and relations, and with reacting to them by means of the various motor and symbolic processes that center in skills, problem solving, and intellectual activity. Almost all phases of this domain show marked increases with age which are readily measured. Moreover, they are significantly related to the efficiency of the mature person. It is in this area that society by concentrating its formal educational procedures makes possible the accomplishment of the adult. Within limits, often determined by genetic factors, progress depends upon the amount and type of learning that is done.

As we view the growing person as a system, we may emphasize either biological needs or orientation toward stimulation. We are now swinging back to an emphasis upon the infant as stimulus-oriented, that is, as seeking more and more stimulation within moderate ranges of quality and intensity. In an earlier day psychologists referred to the curiosity and manipulation of the infant, to his positive reaction tendencies, and to the principle of ambience. These views see the infant not as a passive being concerned only with the satisfaction of biological needs, but as an active mobile person very much interested in the objects in his environment. Through this outward searching and the contacts with a wider environment, much of what we know as human, as distinct from animal, behavior evolves. Out of stimulus-orientation and spontaneous or play activity superimposed upon the need reduction of appetites the human being builds his complex life as a person. Involved is an elaboration of activity through perceptive and symbolic processes, reinforced by the ability to retain earlier experiences. In this elaboration communications and relations with other persons play a great role. As the infant is transformed into the free moving and communicative child, life with all its manifold possibilities of interest, activity, and social life opens up. And biological needs are channeled. Free locomotion, the agile hand with thumb opposition, the flexible throat with its variety of sound, added to the child's curiosity and manipulation, lead to a search and exploration of the environment that creates a new world for him and for other children.

The Environment of the Child

Naively we think of an environment as consisting of specific stimuli which occur once and produce immediate response. But when observations of children in their natural habitat were made by Barker and Wright, by following children and recording their behavior from early morning until late at night, a different picture was obtained. In the small Kansas town, there were some 2,030 different settings made up of behavior objects to which children were called upon to react. By various sampling techniques Barker and Wright estimated the total number of behavior objects to which the normal eight-year-old child can react and came out with a figure of 1,200,000. This figure should give us pause, as it indicates the tremendous number of differential responses already built up out of the high intake and high outgo at a comparatively early age. Some 2,200 distinct transactions involving some 660 different behavior objects occur during a 24-hour period. The child is in about 150 different learning situations during a waking day, many of which are outside of the formal school situation. Moreover, experience has a marked repetitive quality when observed from day to day. Children when told to do a thing once do not proceed to do it, but rather arrive at organized behavior through iteration and reiteration: in other words, through time and practice. Multiplying these daily figures by seven for a week or 30 for a month or 365 for a year will give an idea of the flow of transactions through the child as a system.

Some attention should go to the recent work of Hebb and

his associates. On restricting the amount of stimulation received by humans and animals to minimal levels, they found quick deterioration in behavior and activity. They believe that a certain amount of stimulation, which they call arousal stimulation, is necessary to keep the organism functioning, and that above this level there is the stimulation from specific cues which enables us to perceive objects, persons, and relations, and thus respond effectively to them. This is a kind of psychological tonus, not too different in conception from physiological tonus.

In any event, it is clear that in the living organism there is a high intake and high output of transactions in quantitative terms and that the atmosphere in which the child develops is made up of recurring experiences, attitudes, and emotional episodes which reinforce or extinguish various behaviors. Some recurring situations have a standing or lasting quality in time, while others have a fluid quality or brief existence in time.

Comparable studies of discipline indicate that the behavior of children over time varies with the proportion of permissive versus nonpermissive, or of positive and negative suggestions made by the parent or teacher. This also is a flow concept that leads us to conceive of an atmosphere of iteration. Such observations raise the question as to whether the world of control is a black and white one with a sharp separation between categories, or one of reinforcements and inhibitions which vary in amount over time. The question is also raised whether behavior is as stable as it seems to be;

rather it seems to involve an equilibrium maintained by the relation between input and outgo.

Another school of thought thinks of the child's experiences as made up of episodes which are traumatic and which, therefore, affect behavior over long periods. Sometimes attempts are made to trace later behavior back to such episodes in the early years. But others regard the events that impinge on the child at one period as a sample of the events which are likely to occur throughout development. Thus emphasis goes to the consistency of the parents' reactions over time. This view holds that a good mother does not suddenly become a poor one, but rather shows the same quality as a mother when her children are in infancy, childhood, or adolescence. There are unexplored problems in this area, especially when we move away from the stimulation of the moment to the effect of atmospheres and practices over time.

An important aspect of stimulation concerns the feedback received by the child from his environment. The child has eyes and ears. He not only senses what happens directly around him, but he also observes the effects of his actions upon others and modifies his behavior accordingly. Success elicits favorable responses and failure negative responses from others. If the child is continually frustrated, he will in time react not only to the same stimuli as are received by other children from objects and persons, but also to the manner in which others reject him. Thus the delinquent child reacts not only to the objects which he steals or destroys, but also to the fact that other people knowing of his delinquency expect him to be so. Similarly, the child interested in a particular activity builds up skill which by attracting the attention of other children or of adults leads him to build up more skill. Thus there is a dynamic series of relations with a social overlay in which expectancies of various types modify and change behavior. Many of these relations are circular and reverberating. Therefore the child and the environment cannot be conceived as two sharply separated and distinct entities, but as parts of a field in which there is continuous interaction. Improving the behavior of children may involve modifying the behavior of their parents, their associates, and their teachers quite as much as it involves changing the behavior of the child himself. Thus we seek knowledge about positive and negative feedback from the environment.

Out of studies of infants has come the view that the infant and young child need much stimulation and much affection during their early years in order to promote their mental growth and development. On the one hand this problem has been approached by asking how young children who are deprived of much or of particular types of stimulation develop, and by asking how enhancement of stimulation promotes development. In the former area much experimental work on animals is now going forward and there is still controversy. The problem here is one of separating the effects of sensory stimulation from those of affection and both of these from those of contact with a particular person, the mother. Early it was found that gentling or handling the animal infant improved his adult behavior. This was interpreted as satisfying an emotional need. Then experiments in which stimulation was given mechanically produced similar adult outcomes, suggesting that it was the sensory stimulation rather than emotion which produced the result. Recent work by Harlow and his associates demonstrates that infant monkeys given bodily contact with a satisfying surface show better development in most aspects of overt behavior and that such contact is more effective than the nursing of the animal, which would be expected to affect such outcomes. I have emphasized animal rather than human studies because they bring the controversy into sharper relief. But both are leading to a systematic exploration of the environment of the young.

At later age levels studies have shown the different effects of control procedures depending on the personality of the mother. A warm mother can maintain stricter discipline without harm to the child than can a cold mother; whereas with a cold mother, less discipline seems to be better. Thus an analysis of the effectiveness of techniques for nurturing children must consider both the procedures used for control and the emotional atmosphere in which the control is exerted. What seems, on the surface, to be a simple and direct relation, must in fact be analyzed as a complex of factors.

Suppose that we deal with children who have been exposed to very bad environments. What do we know about the types and amount of stimulation which, given later, will repair or compensate for deficiencies in early stimulation? Some data indicate that these children at later ages show under comparable conditions more rapid rates of learning and more effective learning. Studies of individual children exposed to incredible experiences during World War II, or who have met terrifying experiences in ordinary living, sometimes reveal amazing recoveries with competent and happy living at later age levels. Other studies do not show such effects. What is the nature of the "self-repair mechanisms" which operate when external stress is removed and how can the environment be given an appropriate stimulating quality? We know little about the mechanisms of recovery from psychological stress. Because effective self-repair mechanisms exist for many physical diseases, medicine often thinks that its function is to make it possible for the person to cure himself. For both theoretical and practical purposes, we need knowledge of how stability is re-established and how good adjustment emerges after stress. It is quite clear that the normal child has substantial capacity to withstand stress, that he recovers quickly from short term deprivations, and that he has great capacity for self-repair and adjustment.

Development and Age

After describing the child as an energy system, we return to development. Although changes with age are not striking when observed over very short periods of time, they are very great over a long period. A young child seems almost like a different person when we see him after a few months absence. As the child grows and interacts with objects and persons, it becomes difficult to separate out the results of maturing from those of learning and from the cumulated skills and knowledge in the repertoire for meeting life situations.

Studies of development show significant progress with age in perception, in skills, and in knowledge no matter where we dip into them. In emotional traits and in motivation age changes are not as great. This suggests that there may be age-bound and age-free traits and that there is some separation between the energy, motive power, or drive of the organism and the manner in which the energy available to him is manifested in activities.

Development is not uniform throughout all phases of mental life. For each process there are differences in rate, in the age at which acceleration occurs, and in the age at which the terminal point is reached. Nor is development merely a matter of adding inches to stature, or ability to ability; instead it is a complex process of integrating many structures and functions. In some areas the person grows rapidly in infancy, slowly in childhood, and little in adolescence; in others he grows slowly in childhood and rapidly in adolescence; whereas in others the rate is fairly constant throughout childhood and youth. But overall, the rate of change tends to be greatest in infancy and early childhood and least as the person approaches adulthood.

Examination of the interrelations found between the various aspects of growth indicates that at any level the child, both physically and mentally, exists in his own right and is, therefore, to be understood in terms of the developmental level he has reached rather than as a miniature adult. A common error in the popular and scientific literature on children involves projecting adult processes or states backward and assuming that children possess the characteristics of the mature person. For example, care should be taken in projecting the anxiety or aggression typical of adults backward and assuming that children's behavior, which superficially resembles it, has the same origin or character. Similarly, we cannot assume for scientific and practical purposes that the intelligence of the child is precisely the same as that of the adult. This adultomorphic fallacy often leads to grave error.

As we study the development of children, we find that virtually every process changes in some degree and remains stable in some degree. The extent of change and of stability has to be determined by appropriate studies. The growing person is not a static creature with much fixed behavior, but an adaptable system that acquires many skills and much knowledge with which to move into adult life. Moreover, in the absence of pathology, he retains his learning capacity throughout adult life and well into old age.

In a discussion of age changes a word of caution should be inserted. Although all persons develop along much the same course, there are, nevertheless, marked differences between individuals in their capacities and in the rates and manner in which they develop. Some have more resources, some have fewer; some develop faster, some more slowly. But all move toward maturity. In practical programs we need to know not only where the child is in the age progression, but also the level of his capacities and skills.

DEVELOPMENTAL TASKS. As the child grows, he encounters

a series of tasks of which some are put to him by his environment and some by his internal growth processes. There are events which by changing the relation of the child to his environment acquire significance. The first such event is birth, when the child emerges from an environment in the mother's womb that is quite constant and of low stimulating value, to the variable and highly stimulating external world. A little later when the child begins to walk, he changes from a person tied to a particular spot to which stimulation must come, into an active, free-moving organism that can explore his environment and create his own stimulation. Although walking is internally initiated and appears universally within a narrow age span, the child who walks faces the problem of adapting himself to a new world of space and of developing a large repertoire of new perceptual and motor skills. This will take many years.

Similarly, the appearance of speech changes the child from an animallike person who can respond only to signals into a person who, with symbols at his command, can condense and symbolize experience, store memories, and influence other people. While the transition to symbolization takes place quickly, the development of competence in verbal and communication skills takes many years and affects many areas of living. Still later a great transformation takes place at puberty when the child moves into adolescence and becomes sexually mature. This transition gives the child new interests and powers and radically changes his orientation to life.

But there is another developmental phenomenon which

is geared to the demands of society. At six society requires the child to attend school, to learn to read, and to manipulate numbers. For a number of years thereafter he will be acquiring competence in these and related skills. While the acquisition of these skills is slow and the demand comes from outside, nevertheless, there is a transition into a new area of competence and a substantial enlargement of the life space. Many later skills depend upon reading ability and upon numbers in much the same sense that many motor skills depend upon locomotion. We should also point out that within each of the broad areas of development, whether orginating in internal impulse or social demand, similar transformations occur. For example, within intellectual development there is a transition from concern with the concrete to concern with the abstract.

Paralleling these transitions to new levels of competence is a somewhat similar developmental course with respect to appetite control. In early life the child learns to control his appetites by acquiring various habits of eating, eliminating, and sleeping. In acquiring these controls, the basic problem is that of ordering internal impulses, which have their own natural cycles, to living in a society which sets its own cycles and determines much of the behavior through which the appetite is met or channeled. Present studies stress the importance of developing this behavior at an appropriate time in the life cycle under skillful training with good models and without too rigorous control. Since the demands of different appetite systems may be parallel, the child may be working on various control systems at the same time. At one time strictness in scheduling and training was emphasized; then came the period of self-demand and easy training; now we are in a period of consolidating the two approaches.

If we look at these phenomena for common features, we find a new and partially organized pattern of response, arising as a result either of internal process or of external demand. There follows a period in which the emerging process itself becomes organized. This involves the acquisition of new skills and orientations. Then competence or maturity with respect to the process in question is followed by a movement to new experiences with enlarged power and greater freedom.

In a sense the growing person is continuously achieving freedom to meet new zones of experience. After competence is obtained in one area, the situation, problem, or event loses its problem character and is met by routine or semi-automatic behavior. This process of automatization or ritualization is an important phase of development as it permits the growing person to push problems behind him as he advances. These phenomena become closely tied to age and can be readily plotted in our age-graded society. But there is also an hierarchy of level and content in the demands at various ages. The best example is the school curriculum which locates its subject-matter at particular age levels and expects the child to follow a normal course in acquiring skills and controls.

Because the children of any particular age level are moving along together, and because children differ among themselves, pressures develop among children to conform to the pattern. Children know each other as friends and rivals; their parents have expectancies and compare them with other children. To be accelerated is to receive acclaim; to be retarded is to receive blame and to develop feelings of guilt. The child who fails to make normal progress and who grows up among his fellows who are at the same age levels is put under unusual pressures. Thus we have thwarted, blocked, retarded, and handicapped children within each area who need special treatment to meet life's problems. The attack is twofold: first, to normalize their progress through the developmental course by special assistance at critical periods, and, if normal progress is not possible, to see that they attain as much competence as they can within the limits of their own nature. Involved in either type of adjustment is the problem of lessening the feedback from age peers and adults which has harmful effects in that the child reacts, as was pointed out earlier, not only to the situations presented to the normal child, but also to the knowledge of his own inadequacies among others. Thus children who are retarded or delayed in development live in a different psychological environment than do normal children. Although this is also true of the accelerated child, the feedback is not as bad as it is much more likely to be positive than negative.

To adapt the child to the demands of our life and to give him the skills necessary to meet them, we instruct him. From the developmental point of view, the major problem is to provide instruction at appropriate points in time. This is not only the point at which the child is ready for instruction, but also the point that will anticipate his need for the skill in the life situation. Since each child learns within the framework of his developmental level and capacities, it follows that the parent, teacher, or coach is guiding an internal process rather than imposing a pattern. In order that learning go forward, there must be opportunities for practice under high motivation with knowledge of the results.

The process of acquiring controls and skills is relatively slow; it is spread out in time and involves many errors on the part of the learner. It moves ahead best in an atmosphere of patience, forbearance, and understanding. The most important point to keep in mind is that out of the fumbling, inaccurate, and inadequate attempts of the beginner there comes the skill, competence, and mastery of the expert. In the early stages there are many reversals and difficulties. Hence, too early and too rigorous emphasis upon accuracy, error, or minute detail may cut the motivation of the child and limit the possibilities of learning. In the early stages of learning a good model of the behavior desired with primary emphasis upon the pattern and praise for successes is effective. As practice goes forward, more emphasis can go to smaller units, details, and criticism. In fact, many children reach a stage at which they voluntarily seek criticism as they come to understand its relation to performance.

In some respects the development and the learning resemble each other in that the child is in the process of becoming. Hence those responsible for children should be more interested in progress than in the status of the child at any particular moment. It is not so much perfection in the immediate moment as the likelihood that the child will respond better later on that should govern the actions of parents and teachers. If the child is moving ahead and is responsive to his own internal demands and to those of society, those responsible for him can have confidence in the outcomes.

Several other aspects of the course of development are important. One relates to the manner in which the person classifies and orders his experience in order to operate in the world of objects and persons. The external world is very complex in terms of the amount and variety of stimulation. Even though the child is positively oriented toward stimulation, he must simplify it in order to manipulate it. For example, he learns to call objects of certain shapes "chairs" by ignoring their color and reacting to their form and use. He learns to see a human figure at varying distances from his eye as of a constant height, irrespective of the fact that persons farther away subtend a smaller visual angle. He learns to hear spoken words clearly, even though they vary widely in pronunciation and inflection. In his motor behavior he moves toward economy by simplifying action. These processes not only facilitate his perception and reaction, but they also make it possible for him to react to a greater range and variety of stimulation. As a result, the adult lives in a structured and ordered world in terms of the interrelations of its parts.

A second principle relates to the selectivity of the person. When life begins, the person is a unique pattern of traits which have come down to him from his ancestors. He faces a complex environment in which his experiences and learning will differ from that of any other person. As he faces experience, he chooses activities that are congruent with his own make-up and his developmental level. With age and the organization of behavior, selection becomes apparent. Studies show that the child at eight or nine years has the widest range of interests and activities and that as he grows older his range of interests narrows. However, his concern with particular interests becomes greater. Thus life in its early stages becomes literally an exploration in which various activities are tried and some are selected. Studies also show that children select their chums and companions in terms of the presence of abilities and interests that resemble their own. For example, brighter children select older and duller children select younger ones as companions. As children develop, these tendencies become more marked. As a result, social groupings of all types show more homogeneity at later than at earlier ages. Vocations and recreational activities, with their hurdles and training requirements, carry the selective process still further.

Our information on selection suggests that we should set up environments that permit a wide range of activities in the earlier years. There are two reasons for this. Since traits and abilities show low correlations with one another, it follows that the person needs to explore himself and his environment in order to determine his potentialities. Next, since the process of development is one of organization in which simple units are put together into more complex patterns, it follows that a broad base of experience will facilitate higher levels of final organization. A rich and varied environment offers better possibilities for selection than does a limited and narrow one and permits the person to move from breadth of concern to depth of concern.

The Concept of Maturity

From the analysis of the developmental course there emerges a concept of maturity. Although maturity is defined in various ways, there is a common basis of agreement, despite the fact that adults, even when very well adjusted, are not equally mature in all respects. For example, some adults are primitive in their thinking in one area while quite advanced in another, and persons who are competent in some phases of life may be emotionally immature in others.

A mature person is one who, having met many problems, has developed a range of competencies which enable him to meet those of adult life. From his experiences he has acquired some capacity for independent action, for making his own decisions, and for controlling his emotions. He subordinates the satisfaction of some impulses in order to accomplish more worthy purposes. Because he tends to be task-oriented rather than self-oriented, he can work with and feel with others in spite of their inadequacies and imperfections. He meets problems, solves them, and moves on without prolonged emotional disturbance. Thus an ability to bounce back and to repair oneself, added to the capacity to remain stable and wholesome in the face of the complexities of living, marks a well-adjusted and mature person. The goal of development is then the orderly, persistent, and responsible behavior out of which comes efficiency and power. It is assumed that if the emerging life pattern is coordinated with the capacities and goals of the person, happiness will become an aspect of maturity.

Questions of maturity can be raised about all persons, adults or children. Is the child advanced or retarded in comparison with others of his age level in meeting particular problems? In the areas in which he is immature, what experiences and opportunities can help him to eliminate or reduce his immaturity? Does the environment give the child opportunities to acquire competence? Or is it of such a nature that the child is in constant difficulty? Some environments are continuously frustrating in the sense that no matter what the child does, he cannot move forward. Other environments are facilitating, even though they present difficult problems. To be facilitating there must be a way through the difficulty by learning appropriate skills. For example, a frustrating environment for the adolescent with respect to social life would be one in which every attempt on his part to mingle with his fellows on his own is discouraged, either by direct command or by an attitude such as viewing sociability as abnormal, not as normal. On the other hand, a facilitating environment would be one in which high values were placed on cooperation with one's fellows, in which social relations were taken as a matter of course, and in which facilities for relations with others were available.

Progress toward maturity then, depends in some degree

upon the freedom given children or youth for growing. But it also depends on the availability of support for growing. In an appropriately designed environment the child's efforts to develop will be encouraged. Those about him will not be quite so much concerned with his occasional failures or inadequacies as with his successes and triumphs. They will give him feelings of accomplishment as he meets problems and builds skills. It will not be so demanding or so emphasize perfection that no matter what he does it will be wrong, nor so easy and slip-shod that anything goes. It will be facilitating rather than frustrating and thus give freedom for growth.

The Self-Concept and Personality

In discussing the manner in which an environment that will facilitate development can be conceived, we must not forget the person's own conception of his relationship to life. From the tenor of our discussion it is clear that development within our society is thought of as a transition from external to internal controls. The outcome of socialization, or our way of adapting the impulses of the child to the demands of society, is an internalization of motive in which self-control largely replaces external control. In such a view, emphasis goes to attitudes, goals, and value systems as revealed in the person's concept of himself.

Through his experience the child comes to conceive of himself as a particular kind of person. He gains some awareness of his own competence and of his skill patterns. He develops sensitivity to the values others place upon his efforts. He reacts to the values in the atmospheres of his home, his school, his community, and his country. He responds to group pressures. He develops aspirations and ideals.

There are three major aspects of his personality: his skill and competence as shown in his accomplishments, the effect produced by his behavior on other persons, sometimes referred to as his social stimulus value, and his conception of himself. While these aspects are interrelated, they are far from perfectly correlated. When we try to trace the origins of the elements in the personality of the mature person, we have difficulty, whether we concern ourselves with skills and knowledges or with attitudes and value systems. Much attention in our society goes to the formal instruction centered in our schools. Some goes to informal instruction given in the home, where children observe the reactions of the mother, father, and the other children to and among themselves, see and hear how the parents act toward the neighbors, and are present when guests selected by the parents are entertained. The child is also a member of a family which lives in a particular neighborhood, belongs to a particular church, has a political viewpoint, subscribes to particular magazines, and so on and on. From these sources material comes down to the child through informal discussions and osmosis rather than formal instruction. It is within this framework that many attitudes and beliefs are formed.

If, however, within this framework, the child becomes more attached to one parent than to the other, to one teacher more than another, or if in his reading or in his viewing of television he selects particular characters as his heroes, attachments develop that are likely to increase the effect of stimulation from a particular source. Thus what psychologists call identification makes both formal and informal instruction more effective. Children need heroes with whom they can identify. They need persons who by giving them a pat on the back from time to time give them emotional reinforcement. They also need people with whom they can talk freely. Some of the factors which lead to sex typing, to occupational choice, and to the development of long-time interest patterns reside in this area.

What may be emphasized, however, in considering these phenomena is a continuing contact over time. If a single experience is to be effective, it must in some way modify the stream of practice or affect the current of social relations. Even where single and sudden experiences reorganize behavior, it is possible that the person has been prepared in advance by his previous experience. What we seek then is knowledge of how to eliminate destructive components and to reduce negative components, while we increase the positive stimulation given the child.

In the past research has been much concerned with limited environments operating over short periods. Now that we are making longitudinal studies of children, the effects of longer lasting environments are emerging. We now write descriptions of what to do for children less in terms of stimuli that operate for a short term and more in terms of those that operate over long periods. We now look forward to being able to describe in some detail atmospheres and the sources of stimulation that will affect the later behavior of children and youth. Much study now goes to deprived and restricted environments. Many are concerned with the education of retarded, normal, and bright children by enriching the environment. Thus we attack from converging angles.

Conformity and Independence

But lurking in the background is the central problem of the modern world. Obviously, as we know more and more about patterns of stimulation, we increase our control over outcomes. What are the political and social outcomes if such controls are exercised for poor purposes? This problem was put in striking fashion by Aldous Huxley in *Brave New World* and by George Orwell in *1984*. It is discussed in many popular books and has received professional attention. No immediate and easy solution appears.

But two basic assumptions become clear if we approach this controversy from our American ideals. The first is that we are not primarily concerned with imposed patterns, but with establishing environments that will make it possible for the individual to preserve his identity as a person by freedom to establish his own patterns. Thus we seek personality development and enhancement rather than conformity to a prescribed pattern. But even in a modern democratic society this takes some doing since every person is surrounded by masses of informal stipulation which move him toward conformity. Second, it is clear that in the design of our training program we need to foster self-reliance, responsibility, and independence, while at the same time we encourage cooperative relations with others.

But because society as a system needs a continuing stream of new ideas, we must also encourage unusual personality types—the "other" types of mind. From the long-time point of view we seek fertility of ideas and a continuing new look at experience, even while we are engaged in preparing persons to meet the specific roles upon which a complex and interlocking society depends. Emphasis goes, then, to freedom and responsibility rather than to conformity and dependence upon a central figure.

In conclusion, we may return again to the movement from the dependence of infancy to the independence of adult life, with which we began. A living organism is a very complex system maturing within a complex environment. Whatever may be our views about the genetic limits within which development occurs, the fact remains that it is the environment in and with which we work in order to improve the well-being of children and the adjustment of adults.

How then can we, in the broadest sense, characterize a desirable environment in relation to the early years? In our terms, it is one that is rich in the sense of stimulation, and supporting in the sense of affection. It is one that permits identification with models of desirable behavior. It is one that gives the child an opportunity to develop stable behavior patterns by not being erratic and inconsistent. It is one that enhances rather than degrades personality. In a phase, it is one in which the primary concern is building up the child's confidence in his environment.

Then comes puberty with its marked changes in orientation toward life. The child, now an adolescent, begins to move away from the home. Within a few years he will be on his own and take on the responsibility for his own family. Our task with adolescents is to facilitate the movement from the security of childhood to the responsibility of adult life. If the early home environment is concerned primarily with building up the child's confidence in his environment, the essential task of the home environment of the adolescent is that of building up his confidence in himself. Self-reliance does not develop in a vacuum, but comes through opportunities for making decisions and for participating on one's own in meaningful activities. Opportunities should come first in small degree, later in large degree.

What we have here described as two types of environment, one for children and one for adolescents, is not as bipolar as our language suggests. Throughout development we are concerned with transformations in time. These sometimes occur in a short period, sometimes in a long one. These transformations vary with age level and with individual differences. Hence, we emphasize insight into and understanding of the child's capacities, and of his level of development. Our goal is to transform the child's confidence in the environment gradually into the confidence in himself that enables the adult to meet life with zest and vigor.

EDUCATIONAL OBJECTIVES OF AMERICAN DEMOCRACY

by R A L P H   W .   T Y L E R

IN THE EARLY days of our nation free public education was strongly advocated and eventually established. In the debates over this step two primary purposes of education were emphasized. For the individual child education was to provide the opportunity to realize his potential and to become a constructive and happy person in the station of life which he would occupy because of his birth and ability. For the nation, the education of each child was essential to provide a literate citizenry. Since the new nation was ruled by its people, ignorance among the people threatened the survival of the country.

Today, these remain two of the educational objectives of our schools, recognized by the public generally and firmly embedded in the thinking of educators. But since 1870 we have added three other objectives. As the tide of immigration from Europe reached massive proportions in the latter part of the century and as the children of immigrants be-

Ralph W. Tyler is Director of the Center for Advanced Study in the Behavioral Sciences.

came a considerable proportion of the school population in
several of the states, many of the new citizens began to
perceive the American schools as a means by which their
children might have a fuller life than they had had. Their
children could get a chance through education to get better
jobs and to enjoy other benefits of American life which
they had been unable to do. Hence, in addition to providing
opportunities for individual self-realization and educating
for intelligent citizenship, the American schools have become a major avenue for social mobility, the means by
which the American dream has been achieved by many
thousands of families, and new strains of vigorous leadership have been injected into our maturing society.

The expectation that public elementary and secondary
schools would prepare the workers needed in our expanding
economy was not commonly held until the close of World
War I. Farm laborers, construction workers for railroads and
highways, domestic servants and unskilled "helpers" comprised the majority of the labor force. Skilled tradesmen
came from Europe or were trained through apprenticeship
in this country. But the rapid rate of industrialization and
business development since 1910 required many workers
with higher levels of skills and understanding such as mechanics, stenographers, clerks, and salespeople. The level of
education required came to be expressed increasingly in terms
of a high-school diploma. Furthermore, specific vocational
education was introduced in many high schools with grants-
in-aid provided by the federal government. By 1925, the
public generally and the schools as well were including

as one of the objectives of American education the preparation of young people for the world of work.

Since 1925, and particularly since World War II, the rapid rate of technological development in industry and agriculture has so changed the occupational distribution of the total labor force that the chance for a youth or young adult without high-school education to obtain employment is less and less. Farmers and farm laborers who made up 38 percent of the labor force at the turn of the century now comprise about one-tenth and the Bureau of Labor Statistics predicts a further reduction of nearly 20 percent of the present figure during the next ten years. Similarly, opportunities for employment in unskilled occupations have dropped sharply and are continuing to diminish. The percentage of the labor force employed in skilled trades is not likely to increase. But there are large increases in the percentage of people employed in science, engineering, health services, recreation, administration, accounting, and controlling, and the changes are accelerating. The Bureau of Labor Statistics estimates that during the next ten years the labor force will grow dramatically, increasing by 13.5 million, and during this period, 26 million new workers will enter the labor force, 37 percent more than during the 1950s. Not only is high-school education essential for most employment but the percentage of jobs requiring college education is increasing at a rapid rate. Education as preparation for employment is more important than ever before.

To maintain and to increase the productivity of the American economy require not only an ample supply of workers at higher levels of competence but also consumers who want and are willing to pay for the wide range of consumer goods and services which the economy can produce. If the American people wanted only food, clothing, and shelter, a major fraction would be unemployed because these goods can be produced by a small part of our labor force. The desire and the willingness to pay for health, education, recreation, and other services create the demand which enables the economy to shift its patterns of production to take advantage of the greater efficiency of technology, without stagnation. This sets a fifth major objective of American education, namely, to develop in students understanding and appreciation of the wide range of experiences, services, and goods which can contribute much to their health and satisfactions. Only through education can people learn to make wise economic choices as well as wise choices in the personal, social, and political fields.

This increase in the number of objectives which the American schools are expected to attain is the natural result of the changes in our whole society. In the nearly 200 years since this country was founded, society has increased enormously in complexity. Yet today, the human individual at birth does not differ appreciably from the babies born at the time of the American Revolution. All of the knowledge, skills, and attitudes required to live in modern society must be acquired by each individual after birth. Since society is continuing to increase in complexity and scope, the development of youth for effective modern life increases in difficulty and in magnitude with each generation.

The Basic Tasks of the School

Up to the present, the American schools have been amazingly effective in assuming these increased responsibilities but their spectacular success is a major source of present difficulty. Whatever the educational demand of the moment— driver education, elimination of juvenile delinquency, "air age" education, swimming and other sports, specific vocational skills—the American public views their schools as not only capable of assuming successfully almost any conceivable task of education or training but also as the proper agency to undertake any such job that seems important to some group. No clear basis which the schools can use in selecting among the tasks is commonly recognized in America.

Discussions of this problem are frequently confused by arguments regarding the values of learning to drive safely, of wholesome recreation, of appreciating the contributions of aviation, of learning to swim and to participate in other sports, and of acquiring specific occupational skills. These are not the primary issues facing American education. Many of the jobs the schools are urged to do are worthwhile and many of them the schools can do effectively. The essential point here is that the total educational task involved in inducting youth into responsible adulthood is far too great for any one of our social institutions to undertake effectively. Only by the fullest utilization of the potential educational efforts of home, church, school, recreational agencies, youth-serving organizations, the library, the press, motion pictures, radio, television, and other formal and informal activities can this nation meet its educational needs. The educational task is a tremendous one which can only be met by the enlistment of all relevant resources. Failure to encourage and to help other institutions to bear part of the responsibility inevitably weakens our total social structure and reduces the effectiveness of our total educational achievements.

Yet this is what we do when we in the schools assume responsibilities which can be discharged by others. Reduced working hours give many adults time to teach driving, swimming, and the like. Churches and other institutions are seeking channels through which to serve youth. Many industries are able to provide on-the-job training. Few, if any, communities adequately utilize the educational potential available outside the school. Instead, they waste the precious resources of the school on jobs which others can do. It is clear that two things are necessary: We need to organize community understanding and leadership for a wide attack upon the total educational job, and we must clearly differentiate the educational responsibilities of the school from those of other agencies.

In identifying the tasks which are particularly appropriate for the school, its special characteristics need to be carefully considered. One major feature is the fact that its teachers have been educated in the arts and sciences. Frequently this characteristic is played down or overlooked because subject matter has often been viewed as dead material—a collection of items to be remembered but not a vital ingredient in life itself. Too frequently we have failed to identify the constructive role of the arts and sciences in education. Prop-

erly understood, the subject matter of these fields is not
dead but can be the source of a variety of understandings,
values, abilities, and the like which aid the student in living more effectively and more happily. The school should
be drawing upon these resources to enrich the lives of the
students.

This viewpoint emphasizes college and university education in the arts and sciences as a primary resource for the
high school to use, but this is a valid position only in so far
as the contributions of the arts and sciences are used as vital
means of learning and not as dead items to recall. This can
be done and often is. All of us can think of illustrations
of the way in which each of the major fields of science
and scholarship can provide things that open up avenues
for living. In science, for example, the kinds of problems
with which the scientist deals in seeking to understand natural phenomena and to gain some control over them, the
methods that scientists use for studying problems, the concepts they have developed for helping to understand the
phenomena with which they deal, the data they are obtaining about various natural phenomena, and the generalizations
which they have developed for relating factors and for ex-
plaining phenomena, all give us tools for understanding our
natural world and for seeking to gain more control over it.
They also give us a basis for continuing our own study and
learning about natural phenomena long after high school.

In history, to take another example, we find bases for
understanding developments which take place over periods
of time. History gives us methods for studying problems

which involve the time dimension and the interrelations of political, economic, social, and intellectual life. History gives us concepts with which to think about and to understand social change. It gives us data and some generalizations. It can help the high-school student to be at home in a world of change and development and to take an active understanding role in this world.

The other subject fields can furnish similar examples of problems, methods, concepts, and generalizations so important in finding meaning and effectiveness in life. In building the high-school curriculum, the arts and sciences need to be treated as vital means of learning. They must be examined carefully for their possible contributions rather than viewed as matters of rote memorization. Furthermore, the education of teachers in these fields should be effectively utilized. All too often we have employed teachers in jobs that do not draw upon their education. The task of the school is partly defined by this important characteristic: the employment of teachers who are educated in the arts and sciences.

A second significant characteristic is the skill of the school staff in facilitating the learning of students. By and large, teachers are effective in teaching. Their training and experience have been largely focused on it. In addition to these characteristics of the teaching staff, there are three other features of the school to be considered in selecting appropriate educational tasks. The school has special types of equipment and facilities, such as libraries and laboratories. The arrangements of enrollment and attendance in the school permit the organization of learning experiences over a considerable period of time. The school has built a tradition commonly recognized and respected in the community. This tradition includes such elements as impartiality, objectivity, and concern for human values. These are very important characteristics not possessed in equal degree by other social institutions. The kinds of jobs the school undertakes should primarily be those which depend upon these characteristics, since they provide for unique contributions.

Considering these features of the school, several kinds of educational tasks are recognized as particularly appropriate. One of these has already been mentioned, namely, learning which is based substantially upon the arts and sciences. A second is the learning of complex and difficult things that require organization of experience and distribution of practice over considerable periods of time. A number of illustrations will quickly come to mind. Probably reading and mathematics are most commonly recognized as fields in which the basic concepts and skills require careful organization, beginning with simple materials and moving gradually to more complex matters over the years of elementary and secondary school. Clearly, this kind of learning is uniquely possible in the school rather than in the less well-organized conditions of other agencies.

A third kind of educational task appropriate for the school is to provide learning where the essential factors are not obvious to one observing the phenomenon and where the principals, concepts, and meanings must be brought specially to the attention of the learner. Thus the scientific concepts and principles which explain the growth and development of plants are not obvious to the observer of plants or even to an uneducated farm hand. The school can more effectively provide for this learning than can the home or job.

A fourth kind of learning appropriate for the school is where the experiences required cannot be provided directly in the ordinary activities of daily life. Geography and history are excellent illustrations of fields where daily life experience alone is not likely to provide sufficient insight into historic matters and matters relating to places far removed. If young people are to develop an understanding of history, it will require the attention of a specialized agency able to provide materials serving to give vicarious experiences and to organize them effectively. The same is true for geography. We cannot depend entirely upon the informal experiences of daily life to provide these kinds of learning.

A fifth kind of learning particularly appropriate for the school is that which requires more "purified experience" than is commonly available in life outside the school. Students may learn something of art, music, literature, or human relations from the examples commonly found in the community, but where these fall far short of the best, the students have no chance to set high standards for themselves. The school can provide examples for study and enjoyment which represent the best available.

A sixth kind of learning particularly appropriate to the school is that in which re-examination and interpretation of experience are very essential. Our basic ethical values are commonly involved in the daily experiences of youth. Questions of justice, fairness, goodness arise again and again on the playground, in the marketplace, and elsewhere. It is not likely, however, that sheer contact with these ideas will be enough to help the individual youth to develop values that are clearly understood and effectively utilized. The school can provide opportunity from time to time to recall these experiences, to examine them, and seek to interpret them, thus clarifying the meaning of values as well as helping youth to appreciate them more adequately. In the realm of ethical values this type of responsibility will be shared by the home, the Church, and youth organizations, but in the realm of esthetic values it is probably true that only the school is likely to provide the opportunity systematically.

These six kinds of learning which are peculiarly appropriate for the school ought to be strongly emphasized in its program in contrast to other learnings which can be provided by other agencies. There are, of course, educational jobs which are good in themselves but do not require the particular conditions that the school provides. When the school undertakes these tasks, it must either neglect other important things or attempt more than it can do well, spreading itself too thin, and not achieving as effective educational results as it should. Concentrating its efforts upon the educational job which the school is uniquely fitted to undertake and encouraging other community agencies in their responsibilities will greatly raise the educational level of the nation.

Research and Experimentation

The more adequate attainment of the purposes of American education demands not only the concentration of attention of the school upon its core tasks and the strengthening of the educational contribution of the home, the Church, and other community agencies, but it also requires increasing effort to find and devise more effective and efficient means of teaching. The phenomenal growth and increased efficiency of American industry, agriculture, and medicine are due largely to the continued search and research for new materials, new techniques, new ways of organizing and managing the enterprises, and a favorable and receptive attitude to new ideas and to experimentation.

There is sufficient indication in the experiments in military training and education and in the scattered investigations in schools and colleges that search, research, and experimentation can produce significant improvements in the effectiveness of education in the schools. But the public attitude toward research and experimentation in education is very different from the attitude of business, agriculture, and medicine toward these activities in their fields. Hence, only a fraction of 1 percent of educational expenditures is devoted to research and experimentation, and changes in materials, methods of learning and teaching, and organization within the schools are commonly greeted with strong opposition. Educational procedures change slowly and even those which have been shown in a number of schools to be more effective are not likely to be adopted by even half of our schools in less than twenty-five years. For example, educational motion pictures, pupil projects which provide concrete applications of school learning, and work experience tied in with the school program have all been in use more than a quarter of a century and have contributed to the effectiveness of teaching in the schools where they are used, but they are still not used in more than half of America's schools. To achieve the level of educational effectiveness required today, we must find new and better materials, techniques and means of organizing education. The public needs to support and encourage research, experimentation and the adoption of new and improved methods.

Equality of Educational Opportunity

Another essential step to attain more adequately the objectives of American education is to attack more vigorously the problem of equality of educational opportunity in our schools. Mention has already been made of the increasing need to maximize the educational achievements of all children to meet the national demands for educated people as well as to decrease individual frustration and failure. In a society where only a small fraction of educated people are needed, single standards can be enforced without great social loss resulting from the failure of large numbers of children to meet the standard. The individuals who fail can be used as unskilled labor, and the possibility of salvage is a matter of humane concern but is not critical to the maintenance of that society. But our society can follow such wasteful practices only at the cost of the breakdown of our dynamic economy and the onset of political demagoguery. Studies in child development clearly indicate that a great deal of learning is possible for almost all children if means can be found to motivate and encourage them, to arrange tasks that each can accomplish, and to provide other adaptations for the variety of individual differences found among school children.

Not only in the elementary schools but also in the high schools, all youth do not have equal educational opportunity. Success in most high-school courses requires a fairly high level of verbal facility and a background of middle-class experience with books and language. Those youth who do not have this background usually find it difficult to pursue the normal high-school program. Instead of recognizing this situation as a challenge to try to work out ways of helping young people of different backgrounds to achieve the basic objectives of education, the school more commonly guides these students into vocational or other nonverbal programs, not as a means of attaining the liberal objectives of the high school but as a substitute for these objectives. To learn to run a lathe, helpful as that is as a means for earning a living as a skilled laborer, is no substitute for gaining a deeper understanding of what life is about, what science, history, literature, art, and other fields have to offer in helping us to understand our world and gain greater command over it. Probably there has never been a time when it was so important for all citizens to gain intelligent understanding and this need is not met by shifting some students into programs that deal primarily with technical skills and manual facility. Even though it is difficult to reach students whose backgrounds have been limited, this is a responsibility which must be met.

Public Attitudes Toward Education

Since the public schools are controlled by people and the school pupils are the children of the people, public attitudes have a tremendous influence on the quality and amount of public education and upon the direction and amount of effort which youth put into their school work. In general, the American public attitude is highly favorable to education. The great growth in school enrollments and the great increases in the public funds provided for schools and colleges are evidences of the public regard for education. However, this favorable opinion of the importance of education and the common desire to have every youth obtain at least a high-school diploma are mixed with other public attitudes which fail to give the most effective support to the attainment of the objectives of American education.

In most American communities, youth see greater public interest and appreciation for athletic performance and bathing beauty contests than for educational achievements. The attitudes which are expressed by the adults in a community are quite commonly acquired by the children and youth and serve to direct their attention and efforts. If the maximum educational achievements are to be obtained, the attitudes expressed by the words and actions of adults and by television, radio, magazines, newspapers, and movies must serve to reinforce these educational objectives. Otherwise, the distraction of attention and the lessened effort which youth put into their studies will reduce their achievements.

Another inadequacy of public attitudes toward education lies in its superficial vacillations from one emphasis to another. During World War II there was great public expression of concern for the physical fitness of youth and in some states laws were passed specifying the amount of time the public schools must devote to physical education. Since Sputnik an even stronger cry has arisen for more science and mathematics. Each fluctuation of public opinion is capitalized by some "pressure group" to influence the schools to shift their emphasis to the special interests of this group.

Of course, new conditions require new study of the educational program to see that the schools are focusing upon the proper objectives in an intelligent fashion, but the need for more scientists and engineers does not require a neglect of other educational fields. Increasing the amount of time the schools are required to devote to physical education is not necessarily a means of improving physical fitness of youth, and it is certainly not an intelligent means of deciding what educational tasks the schools can best undertake and what tasks are more properly the responsibility of other agencies. Furthermore, each new shift of public concern is commonly associated with attacks upon the adequacy of the schools and these are more likely to reduce the morale of teachers and students than they are to increase the schools' effectiveness. Continuing, intelligent criticism of American education and the schools by the public is a good thing when it takes on the quality of a statesmanlike debate in which consideration is given to the several objectives of the school and to the proper balance among them and among the fields of study.

Another matter on which public opinion periodically vacillates is the emphasis upon "toughness" in school work. A few years age the common parental attitude toward mathematics and foreign languages was one of concern that these subjects were too hard for young people and especially too demanding for girls. Currently the attitude expressed is that school work is too easy and that more difficult subjects and hard work should be required by the schools. What the public fails to recognize is that effective learning requires a task which for each pupil is difficult but one which he can accomplish. On the one hand, the thing to be learned needs to be challenging, something beyond the pupil's present knowledge or skill which demands real effort for him to master. On the other hand, for the pupil to put forth his energy and work hard at the task he needs to feel that he can accomplish it and have confidence in his ability to achieve. Because in every school the children represent a wide range of abilities and backgrounds, a task which challenges a less able student is likely to be too easy for the more able one, and a task which is difficult enough to demand real effort from the more able ones will appear to be beyond possibility of achievement by the less able. What is required is the development of a variety of learning tasks so that every student can push his own achievement beyond his previous performance and so that there is a real possibility for every student to gain confidence in his ability to learn things which are difficult for him.

The effect of the present vacillating attitude toward toughness is to influence the schools at some times to develop educational programs that challenge no one and at other times to develop programs which challenge some of the more able but seem so hard for others that their learning is reduced. A realistic recognition of this situation by the public would help to stabilize intelligent efforts to improve the curriculum and instruction in the schools.

The foregoing illustrations are intended to suggest the importance of public attitudes toward education in increasing the effectiveness of the schools in attaining the objectives of American democracy and to illustrate some of the respects in which the current attitudes hinder rather than help. The generally favorable attitudes of the public toward the importance of education can be strengthened by continuing intelligent criticism based on thoughtful study rather than vacillating expressions of conflicting concerns.

The Role of the Teaching Profession in the Community

Public attitudes toward education are in some degree dependent upon the information provided by the teachers and administrators in the schools or the lack of it. It is fair to say that many schools have not clarified their objectives for themselves and still more of them have not explained to their publics in simple fashion what they are trying to do, that is, what their objectives are and how these objectives are being attained. Without these simple, clear-cut explanations many lay people will have only their own memory of school in their minds and will not understand the great socio-economic changes that are taking place to which the schools must respond. Hence, the teaching profession has a responsibility to explain to the community the basic purposes of the school and its ways of working and why these are important and necessary. What is required is straightforward reporting and discussion rather than glamor stories about matters peripheral to the schools' main job.

The teaching profession also has a responsibility in relation to the other educational institutions in the community. The most important of these is the home. Its function in providing the basic physical and emotional needs of the child is unique. In addition, the home can give encouragement to the child's curiosity in a way that greatly facilitates school learning, or the home may greatly inhibit learning in the school by discouraging or punishing the child's efforts to ask questions, to seek in countless ways to satisfy his curiosity, and to express his active interest in learning. A positive attitude in the home toward problem-solving and the interest shown by parents in seeking new light on questions facilitate the efforts of the school in this direction, whereas the attitude that persons in authority have the answers retards the active learning of the child. The provision in the home of means to explore new areas and to carry on inquiries, such as making available appropriate books, music, pictures, a simple shop, is another important contribution of the home to attaining the objectives which are the school's central task.

The interrelation of home and school in the education of children has long been recognized, and the development of the parent-teacher association is one of the important efforts to share responsibility and to coordinate activities. In some communities where homes fail to meet their educational responsibilities, a two-pronged attack is undertaken.

On the one hand, religious and social agencies are employed to counsel and encourage parents to assume proper educational roles, and, on the other hand, socially minded adults are recruited to serve as parent substitutes so that some of the basic emotional and educational conditions may be provided for children whose homes are grossly inadequate.

In addition to the home, there are other institutions in the community which educate, or miseducate, children. For example, the Payne Fund Study of Motion Pictures and Youth demonstrated conclusively that children get from motion pictures ideas about the world and about life which they retain more vividly than many ideas obtained in school. The effect of motion pictures on attitudes and on conduct is also striking and greater than many school influences. If the ideas that the children obtain from movies are untrue or misleading, if the attitudes and conduct engendered by motion pictures are opposed to those sought by the schools, then our educational efforts will be nullified at those points, and the school's goals will not be realized.

A similar condition exists with reference to many other aspects of the child's environment. An effective and thoroughgoing job of education demands more careful study of the total environment of the children and more effort to control the environment so that it will provide an atmosphere and conditions conducive to the growth and development we are seeking to achieve. In this sense, the school cannot sit idly by, unconcerned with the nature of the community in which its children grow up. It is obvious to many of us that we are derelict in our duty when we permit safety hazards and health hazards to exist in the school neighborhood; but in some respects the psychological, the social, and emotional hazards and conflicts surrounding our young people have more disastrous effects upon them than the health and safety hazards.

The school staff must take a stand on matters which affect the opportunities for the education of the children in the community. The school has responsibility for helping to create and maintain an educative social environment. School people should take leadership in initiating those reforms necessary to provide opportunities for education. In many cases, failure to take leadership in these reforms has meant that, within certain sections of the community, education has largely been nullified.

The particular conditions which limit or deny education to many children in a given community are so varied and subject to such changes that they require continuous study and eternal vigilance. In some cases, it may be the poisoned propaganda of a partisan newspaper that so blinds the vision of young people as to warp their conception of social reality and to dry up the springs of social idealism. In others, it may be the lack of any beauty—trees, parks, music, and art—that sterilizes taste and makes life commonplace. In still others, it may be the overprotection of parents, who fail to give children opportunities for the all-important experiences of self-direction and assumption of responsibility.

Because these limiting conditions are so numerous and are not always easy to recognize, they are not likely to be eliminated or improved unless school people take active leadership. This requires knowledge of education and of child development in order to recognize factors in the environment that are not likely to be recognized by the layman until their devastating effects have become obvious. School people as school people have no more responsibility than have any other citizens for seeking the general reform of social institutions, but school people, by the very nature of their task, do have responsibility for seeking those reforms necessary to improve the opportunities for the education and development of children.

Summary

In this chapter several major points have been presented. With the profound changes taking place in our society since our educational system was established, the objectives of American education have expanded. With this enlargement of purposes the schools have also assumed many tasks which are not central to their role, and they are in danger of spreading themselves too thin. The core task is to arouse and maintain interest and skill in learning those things which involve deeper understanding and the solution of new problems. Having defined this central role, the schools must be encouraged to conduct research and experimentation to find new ways to improve their effectiveness. Particularly, new efforts are needed to achieve equality of educational opportunity and to salvage the wasted abilities and talents of children with limited backgrounds. In this effort to achieve more nearly our educational objectives intelligent constructive public attitudes can exercise important influence and the teaching profession can provide further assistance in its cooperation with the rest of the community. Only by strengthening and coordinating the work of other educational institutions as well as the school can our total educational resources be made adequate to the difficult but essential job ahead.

THE AGE OF SCIENCE

by JERROLD R. ZACHARIAS

WE HAVE ALL been hearing and reading—perhaps more often than any of us finds absolutely necessary—such phrases as "The Age of Science," "The Scientific Revolution," "The Dominance of Science." According to the tempers of our own minds we may find them irritating, or arrogant, or naive. What we rarely do with such phrases, or indeed with any catch-phrases, is to think about what they are intended to mean.

I am a scientist and the word "science" has a certain real meaning for me. To a surprisingly large extent it is the expression of an attitude, and as such it is remarkably hard to define. But the attitude stems from a body of practice and a body of procedures, and these at least can be described and considered.

Let me describe the practice of science as the careful preparation of questions to be put to Nature (or the Universe, or the Real World, or whatever you wish to call it), followed by the strict recording of the replies that Nature appears to

Jerrold R. Zacharias is Professor of Physics at the Massachusetts Institute of Technology.

give to such questions, and the attempt to find order and pattern in those replies. I do not pretend for a moment that I have given here an exhaustive definition of science. It is clear at once that it does not include such activities as those of the astronomer or of the taxonomist, both of whom are undeniably scientists. But it does cover most of the activities I would be willing to call science and with a good deal more trouble than it would be worth in the present context it could be extended to cover the rest.

Now, the very existence of an extensive pursuit of such activities presumes the wide existence of two distinct faiths. The first of these is the faith that there is indeed some sort of orderliness and pattern in Nature and that with the exercise of human intelligence and human ingenuity it can be discovered. The second of these is the faith that out of this kind of pursuit and discovery will come something of value to humanity—something we humans desire and from which we can profit. (There is, I suppose, a third faith—the faith that the Universe or the Real World actually exists but I am quite willing to leave that question to the systematic philosophers and much good it may do them!)

You will notice that these two faiths stand at completely different levels. The faith in order applies primarily to the scientist himself, and makes his work possible. The faith in the value of science applies to society in general; it constitutes the basis of the support that society (knowingly or not) is willing to tender the scientist. And at this moment, in the middle of the twentieth century, both these faiths are widely and generally held.

This may not be particularly surprising, but it is certainly new. In the long history of mankind neither of these faiths has deep roots. The second of them is so recent that we can not yet be certain that it is firmly established; the Scientific Revolution no less than the Industrial Revolution has its Luddites, and it is conceivable that this time they will prevail.

It is not much more than three hundred years since the idea of an orderliness in nature began to dominate men's minds. The Greeks had more than a glimpse of it but the Greeks somehow never managed to learn how to catch hold of it; they did what they could with the intellectual tools they possessed and came quickly to a dead end. After that it was not until the time of Galileo and of Newton that the concept was born again. This time, through the genius of these men and their fellows, to the faith in orderliness there was added a technique of eliciting that orderliness by posing perspicacious questions; since Galileo that has been the method of science and its effectiveness cannot sensibly be challenged.

But if Galileo and his descendants created science, they did little to provide fertile ground for its cultivation. For centuries science remained almost an aesthetic pursuit carried on by the sons of the wealthy and a few others whom the general public regarded as eccentrics. The scientists occupied the status, more or less, that the poet holds today.

In our own country, there was simply no general belief that benefits were likely to accrue from the practice of science. Between Franklin and Gibbs—a lapse of well over a century—America was unable to produce a scientist of even modest stature. Into the early years of this century, this country was incapable of providing an education for a man of scientific bent, or of making use of his services when they became available. When General Electric became involved in the intricacies of alternating current, they were forced to send to Germany for a man who could do the mathematics and even if there had been an American Steinmetz he probably would have made his home abroad.

All this has changed. The methods of Galileo and Newton are no longer novel. They have become so deeply embedded in our modes of thinking that we see them pushed beyond their proper boundaries; they are applied to problems to which they are clearly not appropriate. We take the orderliness of Nature for granted, and we are disappointed when we do not find an equal orderliness in, say, language. We consider it a truism that one finds out about the atom, or electricity, or chemical reactions, by doing experiments and there are some who press ahead anxiously to find out about the Soul in the same manner.

And except for moments of disquiet when it appears likely that science will destroy every one of us, the public usually believes that science provides us with things we want. To the scientist himself this belief seems frequently to rest upon a misunderstanding of exactly what it is the scientist does, but what is most important to the scientist is the fact that the support does indeed exist.

To put the matter in its crudest form, there are more

scientists than poets in the United States today because the people of the United States believe they require, for the satisfaction of their needs, more of the one than of the other. They may be totally mistaken but they believe it, and the community of scientists grows in response to that belief. A hundred years ago the belief did not exist, and a hundred years ago there were a good many more poets than scientists in the United States.

It is for these reasons, and for no others, that I think it is meaningful to say that we do indeed live in an Age of Science. I trust, although I am by no means certain, that there will be found neither arrogance nor naivete in the statement as I have attempted to put it forward. Lest I be charged with an immodesty I do not possess, let me make it clear that I am by no means certain that the Age of Science is the best of all possible worlds. All I insist upon is that it is with us, or we are with it, and we cannot wish it away.

The Scientist

Let me now turn from the Age to the individual and allow me to select the individual of whom I should know the most: myself.

A large part of my life has been spent in learning physics, doing physics, teaching physics and discussing physics; I have been fortunate enough to be able to do this at progressively higher levels. I have done experiments, published my results, and seen them incorporated in the corpus of knowledge within my field of effort. With the passage of time I have

been awarded the privilege of putting certain distinctive letters before my name and others after it. In short I am called
a scientist, and I believe I am one.

What does all this amount to? What do I possess, or
what am I doing, that a person who is not a scientist does
not possess or does not do; what sets me off?

To begin with I possess a body of skills and a body of
knowledge. I am capable of combining familiar materials
into an unfamiliar configuration, to predict with some as-
surance how this new configuration will in general behave,
to recognize particular aspects of the new configuration with
which I am unfamiliar, and to find out something about
these particular aspects. I have done this sort of thing so
often, and studied with such attention similar work that has
been done by others, that I am a living storehouse of information about such things, and I can call upon that information either for my own use or for the instruction of others.

All this is very satisfying, but it is scarcely distinctive in
itself. Change a word or two here and there, and much the
same could be said by any practicing poet, bricklayer, or
baseball player. And whatever in my heart I may believe, I
am not prepared to say that what I do is more edifying, more
noble, or more beneficial than what a poet, a bricklayer, or a
baseball player does. If I did so, I am convinced that all
poets, many bricklayers, and even a few baseball players
would be eager to debate the point with me, and the outcome of any such debate is irrelevant to what I wish to establish. I can afford to concede that they are all more worthwhile than I am without prejudicing my argument.

What I can maintain is that society considers my activities more important, more useful. Among the more influential members of society, this is hardly disputable: government and business incorporate scientists into their councils; colleges and universities give them pride of place. And even in the wider range of the whole democracy it remains so: the average scientist is honored far more widely than the average baseball player or the average poet or the average bricklayer. I do not wish to be crass but I might also point out that he is generally paid better, lives better, and enjoys better credit.

I have my skills, then, and a certain position as a consequence. But I derive something more from my particular set of skills. They are part of a family of skills, and I enter into the life of that family.

As a physicist, I have found it necessary to know something of chemistry, astronomy, and a few other sciences that are directly allied to physics or have been spun off from physics. There are other sciences about which I know less, and some about which I know nothing at all—at least in the sense that I could not give an account of them or pass a respectable examination in them. But in another sense, I am familiar with all sciences. I know how they work. I know what a practitioner of any science is up to. I know the sort of thing he must do to advance his knowledge. I know the criteria he uses to judge whether an act of his has indeed advanced his knowledge, or has merely been a false start or a deception.

Now once again, I have by this established no advantage

over the poet, the bricklayer, or the baseball player. The poet, given a block of marble and a chisel, might well be at a complete loss. But the poet knows fairly well what is on the sculptor's mind when he stands before the rough slab of stone, and the poet will look knowingly upon the finished statue. The baseball player may have no competence before the high-jump bar, but he knows about muscle and sinew and concentration, and he has a far deeper appreciation than the rest of us when he watches a seven-foot leap. All skills come in families, mine no more than theirs.

But my family is the family that is relevant to the Age of Science. What this means is simply that the poet and his skills almost never impinge upon the bricklayer or the baseball player and their skills. These are families that can afford to ignore one another. None of them, today, can ignore science. It affects their daily living and the way the fruits of their labor are distributed. It affects them in the practices of their own skills. Most of all, since they are as deeply embedded in the Age of Science as I am, science affects the very manner in which they think, and reason, and come to conclusions. The poet, whether he knows it or not, has borrowed from science both in the manner in which he makes his poems and in the manner in which he judges them. This does not necessarily make them better poems—I, for one, suspect it makes them somewhat worse—but he is as helpless as I in the matter.

I must repeat that I am not attempting to set up a hierarchy of values. I am writing of the world as it is, and we are all free to wish it otherwise. In the world as it is, my family is more relevant than theirs; I mean nothing more than that.

So far I have tried to be specific. But now I must speak of the delight that I derive from science, and I am not sure that I can make that delight completely clear to someone who has not himself experienced it.

I spend my life looking for the orderliness that I believe is to be found in Nature. Nature herself is not hostile to this business of poking and pushing in which I am engaged, although there are certainly times when an experimental physicist is tempted to believe that natural events are engaged in an immense conspiracy against him. But Nature is neither wily, nor tricky, nor antagonistic. She is something that is much worse: she is passive. And it is exactly that which makes science such an enormously exciting challenge.

The answers are all there—perhaps not the answers to the questions that I am asking, but the answers to the questions I should be wise enough to ask. And the pattern is there. All I have to do is find it. No one and nothing prevents me, or makes it difficult for me. It is entirely, unmistakably, and inescapably up to me. If I am capable, I will make progress. If I am very capable, I will make great progress. If I am inadequate, I will fail, and it is entirely because of my own inadequacies that I will fail.

And because the challenge is so great, the rewards are tremendously satisfying. Every step forward is a triumph of mankind. I can glory not only in my own successes (if I am fortunate enough to enjoy successes), I can glory as well in the successes of my colleagues, and derive excitement merely from an account of them. More than that, I can read accounts of the triumphs of Galileo, or Kepler, or Darwin, and glory in them. I know the challenge they faced, I can feel in my bones and my liver and my intestines their tribulations as they faced the challenge, and at the end of the account I shout "Eureka" as enthusiastically as Archimedes ever shouted it.

This is not a response that is peculiar to me or to scientists. Every human being who has ever faced a problem has experienced the delight, the splendor, of the moment when all the disparate elements suddenly fall into place, when the key is revealed, when the insoluble is solved. The scientist and the mathematician live with such problems, all the more pleasurable, as they are the more subtle and the more resistent to solution. It is their business to meet them and attack them. It is their great reward occasionally to solve them.

I do not deny the existence of other delights—those experienced by the poet, the bricklayer, or the baseball player. The happy man is the man who is aware of them all, and who makes an honest effort to taste them all. I might well propose that the delights of the scientist are richer than some of the others because they are harder to come by—they demand more of the man who would share them. The mountain is a good deal more challenging to climb than the foothill. Perhaps I might go further and express a willingness to believe that the peaks occasionally scaled by the poet, the musician, the mystic are even higher than the highest reached by the scientist. But my own greatest pleasures are the ones I know best, and I would like to share them.

Finally, I must speak of one more characteristic of the scientist's career. The young scientist, more than the young practitioner of any other activity, can expect with some confidence that his work will survive him. It may not be a spectacular survival. He is guaranteed inclusion in no Hall of Fame, however parochial. But some of his work is likely to endure and be useful.

This does not arise out of the nature of the scientist, but out of the nature of science. It is, to begin with, an accumulative process. Every poet, every musician, every athlete, every statesman must begin, to a large extent, anew. He can learn, perhaps, from his predecessors, but the edifice he erects must be his own. The scientist, on the contrary, works within a structure that has been in being for centuries. Foundations have been laid, some rooms have almost been completed (they are never quite completed), and new wings are started in each generation. The new workman may add, or alter, or even help design a whole section, but there is no reason whatsoever that he should attempt to begin afresh, and he is rarely tempted to do so.

And so the man who puts in a single humble nail has contributed to the building, and that nail will continue to be part of the building as long as the building survives. On the man who drove it, it confers a kind of immortality—at least as much as anything can.

The chance of an aspiring scientist to make such a contribution, or more, is a good one. He works with extraordinarily sharp tools, themselves the result of an accumulative process. Setting out to accomplish something, the scientist has all the skills and all the insights of his predecessors upon which to draw. If he needs the calculus, Newton and Leibnitz invented it for him, and generations of mathematicians have given it a cutting edge; it is his to employ. Science is an immensely efficient method for gathering certain sorts of knowledge, and all the power of that method is within reach of the young experimenter or the young theoretician.

These are advantages that are peculiarly the scientist's. The musician who does not write great music is quickly forgotten—and great music is not easily written. The second-rate entrepreneur leaves no mark on the world of affairs. But the second-rate scientist who plods away at an honest experiment, and sets down his results for others to study and build upon, will leave an ineradicable mark upon physics, even if all he has achieved has been to make it possible for a better man to do the same experiment more profitably. I do not set this forth as a particularly laudable ambition, but it can certainly be a comfort.

Education

I have spoken of the Age of Science and of the scientist, perhaps at inordinate length and perhaps not always pertinently so far as my real topic is concerned. What I wish now to discuss is the matter of education in this Age of Science.

Education, I believe, is designed in part to accommodate

the child to the world in which he is to live, and in part to make it possible for that child to make a better world. I have set these down as if they were two distinct purposes, but they are actually one and the same, for the child who does not understand and participate in his world is surely not likely to alter it for the better.

The education which we commonly offer our children today is dominated, for the most part, by the considerations of another era. The Age of Science has affected education both as to method and as to substance. But the effects for the most part have been peripheral: the young student studies a little more science and a little less Greek; he is more likely to reach calculus during his high school years, and less likely to reach Horace. These changes, for whatever they are worth, are a concession to the changing times, but little more. The general educational posture today is very little more than the consequence of what it set out to be fifty years ago; our schools seek to conceal intellectual disparities among their students by giving the intellect as little as possible to feed upon, and at the same time proliferate their playing fields and gymnasiums to the end that physical disparities may be made as obvious as possible.

I do not quite know how and why education shifted from the production of mental competence to the encouragement of baton-twirling. In any case, I am content to leave the work of analysis to others, and to speak only of what I, as a scientist, would like to require of an educational system.

Certainly, an educational system should not be designed

to drop its other concerns in favor of converting all its students into scientists. Nothing the schools could do—not even what they are doing now—would be less desirable. Fortunately, it is also impossible. Science requires a certain temper of mind, and most people would be incompetent and unhappy as scientists, just as most scientists would be incompetent and unhappy as business men, authors, or attorneys.

There is no great need to impress young people into careers in science. The nature of the times in which we live is already assuring us that we will have as many candidates for science degrees as we could possibly use. It may be that they are wildly misused after they have been graduated, but that is certainly a problem distinct from the ones that concern us here.

What I would ask from the schools, however, is an honest effort to convey to all their students some reasonable awareness of what science is, what it does, why it does it, and how it does it. I ask, in other words, nothing more than the poets ask, and have been in some degree getting. An appreciation of poetry is instilled into children from the earliest moment that they are capable of responding to it—at least, this is the intention. It continues through the grade schools, through the high schools, and through college. It is certainly not done with any intention of turning out whole generations of poets and essayists and critics; it is done because of a belief that an appreciation of literature, and a knowledge of literature, are part of the intellectual baggage of any educated man—a belief that a man who has never read Shakespeare is very likely not to have anything worthwhile to say. In this Age of Science, I am equally uneasy about the man who has not read Einstein or Bohr.

But it must be made clear that this "appreciation of science" is possible only to those who have "done" science. Physics, biology, chemistry are, above all, methods of coming into touch with Nature, and they can be comprehended only in the doing. It is not enough to read about them, or hear about them—one must participate.

Let me introduce an analogy that is surprisingly apt. I know the rules of baseball, and I know the rules of cricket; I know something about the history of both games. When I watch a baseball game, I watch it with all my being. My muscles twitch when the batter lets a curve slide over the corner of the plate; I feel the ball burrow into the webbing of the glove when the third baseman lunges for a smash down the line. But when I watch a cricket match, I am merely watching grown men hit hard balls with sticks.

The difference? I played baseball when I was young. I played it badly, and I played it with no great devotion, but from time to time I was out on the field running and fielding and batting, and I therefore have a knowledge of baseball— a visceral knowledge—that is entirely different in kind from the knowledge I have of cricket.

That is the only kind of knowledge of science that is worth having. It comes from working at experiments; from setting out to elicit new knowledge from nature. In this context, I mean by "new" only that it must be new to the seeker. He must honestly be looking for the answers to questions that are truly questions; there is certainly no point at all in what passes for "laboratory work" in most of our schools today where the student, having previously been drilled in the fact that the latent heat of vaporization of water is so many calories, sets about grimly making his data come out to exactly that figure. This is not only not science; it is a total perversion of science. The latent heat of vaporization of water is not very important, and in any case can be found in any reference book. It *is* important that a student learn that data never come out "exactly" to anything, and that all knowledge is approximate knowledge—this is a very useful thing to know and may prevent him from doing foolish things several times in later life.

This in itself would be a net gain, but an honest education in science will profit the student far more widely. He can, to begin with, make himself capable of understanding the world in which he lives—a world upon which science impinges at every moment and in every aspect. But beyond that, he will be in a position to participate in science in exactly the sense that he participates in the World Series. He will be able to follow science intelligently, have at least a glimmer of comprehension of moves that he himself could not possibly have made, and share in the intense satisfaction of achievement and progress.

I find it impossible to put this as strongly as I would like to. The next few years are going to be as exciting for a scientist as any era could possibly be. I believe, for example, that the biochemists and the biophysicists are on the very verge of creating life in test-tubes; that within a handful of years they will be able to combine ordinary substances—atoms of this and atoms of that and atoms of the other—in such a way that the product will be alive. As a consequence, they will begin to gather knowledge about the greatest of all our unsolved mysteries—life itself.

I am neither a biochemist nor a biophysicist. I possess neither the store of knowledge, nor the skills, nor even the overwhelming urge to do the things they do. But because I know what science is and how it works, I shall follow their work with a sense of excitement, of participation—let me say it, a sense of glory—that is forever forbidden to those among us who have never come into real contact with science. And I am ashamed of an educational system that denies this participation to 90 percent or more of our citizens.

I find it equally shameful that these statements I have just made about the production of life in the laboratory can be confused—and will be confused by many who read this—with statements about establishing colonies upon Venus. There is a possibility that some day both statements, in one form or another, will appear upon the front page of the New York *Times*; one will be the statement of a scientist reasoning carefully from his data, prepared to lead another scientist step-by-step through the chain of experiment and conclusion that has led him to his goal; the other will be a statement by a man who, out of ignorance or lust for political power or sheer incompetence, wishes people to believe in the wisdom of appropriating large sums of money for studying space travel. No person with the most meager acquaint-

ance with science could fail to distinguish between the va-
lidity of the two statements. But judging from the hard facts
of experience, the editors of the New York *Times* will be
unable to make the distinction, nor will most of the people
who read the New York *Times*.

Considered in terms of dollars and cents, we cannot afford this kind of ignorance among our citizens any more
than the Age of the Industrial Revolution could afford illiteracy. We have already paid heavily for it. During the war
it was frequently pointed out that the most valuable discovery that science could contribute to the war effort would
be a device that would enable generals and admirals to
distinguish between scientists and people who merely said
they were scientists. There was no such device available, and
for the lack of it we wasted billions of dollars and I do not
know how many lives. And worst of all, the device exists: it
is called education.

We have failed to provide an education in science for our
children, and a large part of the blame for this must fall
squarely upon the scientist.

The complex of education is made up of the teacher, and
the tools with which the teacher works, and the atmosphere
in which he works. I am not concerned about the first of
these. It would be good to pay teachers at least according to
the scale of skilled laborers, and I believe that soon they will
rise to that eminence. Meanwhile, we have them—devoted,
earnest men and women who are teaching the young because they love to teach the young, and are doing it every

bit as well as they are permitted to, and often a little bit better. As for the atmosphere in which a teacher works, I have said something about that and will say more about it later.

The tools with which the teacher works—the textbooks, the collateral reading, the films, his own continuing education, and (in the sciences at least) the laboratory materials—all these must be supplied by the professional scholar. And in the sciences, the professional scholar until a few years ago has simply turned his back on the problem; in many of the sciences he continues to do so.

Let me say this very clearly: a high-school textbook on biology can be written only by a man who does biology. Laboratory experiments in chemistry can be created only by an experimental chemist. Films about physics must be made by physicists. A science teacher who wishes to teach science more effectively must be educated in science, and not educated simply in education.

And when I write that the professional scientist must assume the responsibility for these things, I mean every word of it. I do not mean that a committee of scientists should meet and make recommendations about the textbook that must be written; I mean that one or two or six of those scientists must sit down and write the textbook, and follow it in the schools, and revise it where it does not do what they want it to do, and follow it again through the schools, and, when they have emerged with a product that satisfies them, must be prepared to do it all over again in a few years.

Unless this is done we condemn ourselves to the situation

that now exists: physics, chemistry, biology, and mathematics (and for all that, geography, history, and economics) as they are taught in the schools bear no relation whatsoever to physics, chemistry, biology, or mathematics (or geography, history, or economics) as they are practiced. They are irrelevant to the concerns or the environment of the student just as they are irrelevant to the concerns and the environment of the scholar. They can neither inspire the student nor excite him; they bore and repel him because they are boring and repellent.

And once the proper substance has been provided the teacher, it must be buttressed by every aid to learning that the ingenuity of man can devise. Learning is hard, desperately hard. Learning a hard subject is hardest of all, and science, if it is to be worth its salt, is a hard subject. The teacher needs films and slides and optical projectors; he needs someone to help him with disciplinary and administrative details so he can concentrate on teaching; he needs the psychologists of learning to help him chart his course.

This takes money, but the sums are pitifully small. A few million dollars—say the money that is spent annually to buy costumes and batons for drum-majorettes—will do the job in any one subject. For the national expenditure on driver-training, library science, and coed cooking I would expect that the job could be done for every subject that a high school should offer, sciences and humanities alike.

Perhaps I am an optimist, but I am inclined to believe that the restoration of intellectual substance in education would of itself go a long way toward recreating an atmosphere in which teaching will be possible. If there is a contempt for intellectual achievement in our schools today, it comes at least in part from the fact that shamefully little is demanded in the way of intellectual achievement. The football player is constantly challenged to run faster, hit harder, and react more expeditiously than his followers: as a result not only he but those who cheer him on learn to respect running and hitting and reacting. The student who drones away at the extraction of square roots is never urged to try calculus; he is compelled instead to extract square roots at exactly the pace of the slowest arithmetician in his class and he becomes an object of suspicion if he tries cube roots.

I have been dealing for more than three years with the revivification of high-school physics, and the most heartening aspect of the work has been our growing realization that the students themselves are far wiser than their elders normally suspect. We have given them a difficult course, and one that is designed to strain their abilities to the utmost— to strain the bright student as well as the dull one. We have had our troubles. But the students, on the whole, have taken it in stride.

Let me quote from a report from a teacher in Iowa, and I quote this because it is typical: "I conducted a survey following the completion of the course to see what the kids really thought about it after all the grades were in. Practically all said it was the hardest course they had ever taken, and the same number said it was the best. One girl who received 3 A's and 1 C this year (the C in physics) said that she had worked harder and learned more from the C work in physics than she had ever done in getting an A. She felt that her previous study habits had let her down and her background in math had been shallow since she was able to do A work without really understanding what she was doing."

That girl, I am pleased to say, has learned something from her physics course: she has learned that her community has cheated her out of a knowledge of mathematics, not because she could not do mathematics but because she was never given the chance.

Our children must be given the chance. It is not enough to offer them something called "life sciences" (whatever they may be), or "earth science" (whatever that may be); or to provide for some 10 percent or 15 percent of our students unrecognizable melanges of dull facts and bad technology under the name of physics or chemistry. At the very least, they should be given mathematics as fast as their minds can take it—and right now mathematicians are proving that children can take mathematics with bewildering facility. (Let me digress: quite recently Mr. David Page of the University of Illinois Arithmetic Project was showing me exactly how a certain mathematical concept was presented to fifth-grade students. As he concluded, he said, "Of course, with the children I actually go much faster." He was not being entirely facetious.)

Children should be given, in the grade schools, some general acquaintaince with science. In high school, they should have at least one course a year in science; perhaps an introductory course followed by courses in biology, chemistry, and physics. And all these courses should be prepared by first rate scientists and mathematicians, presented with all the rigor of true scholarship, supported by every teaching device our society can bring to bear. This much is a minimum program for the Age of Science—the least we can offer if we intend to create for all of us, and for our children, a better, happier and more satisfying world.

WASTED TALENT

by HORACE MANN BOND

IN THE MANNER of all institutionalized ideas, the current interest in "wasted talent" carries old concepts over into a situation presumed to present a new challenge, and to require new attitudes and devices. The older concept was that either through the infinite wisdom of God, or the only slightly less miraculous workings of the genes, there were to be found in the totality of humanity a very small number of exceptionally gifted persons. There was little curiosity about the fact that most of these "talented" persons were the children of persons in the upper brackets of the social order; indeed, this was regarded as a matter-of-fact consequence of the nature of their "gifts," and of the mechanism by which social orders existed, whereby special abilities were transmitted and rose to the top. Everyone knew that cream would rise in fresh milk, and everyone knew that high intellectual capacity in human society had the same ingredient of self-rising fat globules. Less attention was given to the fact that once risen, the cream stayed on top, even unto

Horace Mann Bond is Dean of the School of Education at Atlanta University.

the third and subsequent generations. When the fact, and its reverse, was noted, the harsh but inevitable dispensations of God—or of the genes—furnished a final answer. Who would question either the mysterious ways of God, or the mathematical certainties of eugenics?

Consequently the wastage of "talent" has led us principally to deplore the circumstances that side-track the "gifted" on their otherwise certain road to academic glory. Obliged by the vast numbers involved to quantify our knowledge of the nature and extent of ability, we have elaborated short-cut testing instruments in which we repose increasing confidence as revealers of capacity. On the basis of these findings we have projected numerous ways and means to avoid wasting the "talent" so disclosed. We provide scholarships designed to keep the specially able but struggling student in high school and college, and are only slightly dismayed when we discover that most of our prospects for rescue already are well equipped with the financial buoyancy of their economic and social upper class origin. Increasingly we turn to studies of motivation and personality, or to devices such as guidance and counseling. Be it noted that in all of this we are still ringing the changes on the old refrain: that "talent" is a matter of divine or genetic endowment; and that what most needs to be done is to begin with the fact that "talent" is a scarce and limited commodity, and the nation's sake demands the best thought and action calculated to refine methods for discovering and nourishing this very special rarity.

The purpose of this paper is to present some opposite

views. This is a nation founded by intellectuals who infused
eighteenth-century deistic equalitarianism into the docu-
ments they framed to declare the national aspiration. The
founders, and the people they represented in the Conti-
nental Congress, were also the products of a Bible-believing
age. While holding that "All men are created equal," they
interpreted individual differences around them in terms of
the parable of the talents. We do no differently. Reinforced
by nineteenth-century evolutionary and genetic theories, the
theory of unequal creation is in our generation inspired by
religion and science. As is the way of all true believers, to
offer even a mild dissent is to provoke, from the faithful,
enraged response. In a recent parlor conversation with two
highly intelligent persons—one a cultivated New Englander,
a member of the family of a world-famous physicist; the
other, an equally cultivated Zulu professor—I was obliged
to desist from a further, however timid, defense of the
theory of absolute equalitarianism, for fear of precipitating
a scene. Both of my companions became increasingly in-
dignant—almost apoplectic—that anyone should dare explain high intellectual competence, including their own, on
any other basis than that of the magic of the highly superior
genes they carried within their own bodies.

One is tempted to conclude that practically no one in the
United States actually believes that "All men are created
equal," or ever were. The public, like my Zulu professor
and my physicist's-kin, has as solid a faith in genetic inequal-
ity as Calvin and Torquemada had in their credal varieties.

I have no ambition to become a martyr, but I must never-

theless introduce this paper with a confession of faith—
faith in the equal creation of all men. This faith I am quite
prepared to adulterate, to the extent that certain rare prenatal accidents *do* occur; and, even, to include those equally
rare genetic deficits and surpluses and other aberrations that
are the delight of pathologists. The word "talent" is here
used in quotation marks. The etymologists say that we are
receding from the old meaning of the word. Instead of being
thought of, almost exclusively, as a "gift of God," the word
is now being used in the sense of "will or inclination," derived from the Middle English figure of the "inclination or
tilting of a balance."

I agree with Wechsler, who says that while "individual
differences are real and important, they are not nearly so
great as has commonly been supposed"; and with Pressey,
that "Superior abilities are now generally considered so
predominantly a product of innate constitution that certain
'educational' factors, possibly of very great importance in the
growth of such abilities, are overlooked. . . . This paper
. . . presumes to suggest that there may be ways by which
many more 'geniuses' might not only be discovered but even,
to a substantial degree, *made* and brought to fruition."

In short, I believe that potentially high intellectual ability is not rare, nor to be found only in a select, and limited,
group of human beings; on the contrary, I believe that
there is an enormous reservoir of high potential abilities in
our population, that now, for all practical purposes, goes to
waste. The reasons for this wastage, and possible means for
its recovery, are ancillary themes.

The Gene on a Pedestal

The great majority of evidence published on the subject has been used to substantiate the theory that the historic concentration of high ability in very small segments of the population is of genetic origin. The writings of Sir Francis Galton, cousin to Charles Darwin, appearing from 1865 to 1905, came easily to the conclusion that eminent "Men of Science" and of other fields derived from relatively few family lines. Added to the old Biblical parable, the conclusion became irresistible, that the development of more and abler thinkers depended on better breeding.

Numerous similar investigations, inspired by Galton's pioneer work, have since been made in all of the Western countries, and have pointed to the same conclusions reached by him. The voices taking at least a moderate view have not been lacking in stridence; it has been almost fifty years since W. I. Thomas dared suggest that man never inherited culture; he had always to learn it. Nor can John B. Watson be remembered as a shrinking academician; yet all of his icon-breaking could not prevail against the religio-scientific creed of genetically induced inequalitarianism.

It will be recalled that Galton took the fact of occupational superiority to be causally associated with demonstrated genetic superiority. Of his 107 British men of science, 2 were sons of farmers, 1 of a laborer, 43 of business men, 18 of public officials; 34 of professionals, 9 of the nobility; and, to narrow even further the field of choice, the interwoven "blood" lines were numerous. In the stratified British class system of his time, and even of our own, Galton was a bright and shining example of his own theory. The one child of a laborer represented in his scientific galaxy became an argument for biological inheritance; it was scarcely to be thought of that this rarity might as well have been used to prove the weighty influence of the culture.

This is so with the great number of studies of the origins of other men of distinction undertaken and reported by Pitirim Sorokin. These studies of high ability originated in the hypothesis that outstanding performance resulted from genetic combinations. It is an ironic commentary on the nature of bio-social research that precisely the same material can be useful in defending the opposite hypothesis.

Let us review some of these studies. Philiptschenko studied the origin of Russian scholars, scientists, men of letters, and members of the Russian Academy in the eighty years preceding 1910. His findings were that scholars came from "agriculture" (not differentiated among owners, tenants, and serfs) in 7.9 percent and from labor (all kinds) in 2.7 percent of the cases. Men of letters came from each class in 9.6 percent of the cases. Outstanding contemporary scientists came from agriculture in 14.1 percent of the cases and from laborers (including peasants, not further defined) in 3.5 percent. All of the rest came from the upper classes that comprised less than 5 percent of the Russian population during the period studied. Not more than one-fifth of these outstanding Russians came from rural areas, in a time when more than 85 percent of the population lived in rural areas.

Fritz Maas made a similar analysis of the social origins of

German scientists born after 1700 and dying before 1910. Less than a quarter of these scientists came from the "lower classes"; by our contemporary American definitions, a large portion of those so classified would now be regarded as "middle class." Dividing the scientific group into "exact" and "natural" scientists, Maas reported that only 6.1 percent of the "exact," and 1.3 percent of the "natural" scientists, came from what we would now call the true "lower" classes—peasants and proletarians. Maas concluded that, "This can only be explained through the influence of natural endowment," and citing the fact that the comparatively large number of famous statesmen derived from peasant farmers showed the genetic transmission of the "slyness and craftiness of the peasant, which is a characteristic very advantageous for diplomats."

The biographies of outstanding mathematicians assembled by E. T. Bell contain frequent references to "good intellectual heredity." If this list is taken as a fair distillation of the very highest mathematical genius ("talent") produced in man's recorded history up to the beginning of the twentieth century, it provides an interesting index to the differential social sources of "talent" in the ages preceding our own, rough though such an estimate has to be. In the table that follows, we have tried to place these "geniuses" in contemporary occupational classifications, as used by the United States Census; realizing, of course, that the enormous changes wrought by the machine age within the last century have created new social classes, and new distributions of populations within those classes, analogous to the past only by wide and generous estimates of relative status. For comparative purposes, we have also made a rough estimate of the average occupational distribution of the male labor force in pre-industrial Western societies.

We then arrive at the distributions shown in Table I.

From this table, it appears that upwards of 85 percent of mathematical geniuses were derived from what was, at most, not more than the 10 percent of the population that were in the upper social and economic classes. It is here freely admitted that such a distribution can be—as it has been—used to support the case for the genetic explanation of these abilities.

But our subject is "Wasted Talent." National origins are of interest in this distribution. Western Europe, particularly England, France, and Germany, was prolific in the development of notable mathematicians during the seventeenth and eighteenth centuries; but it was not until the nineteenth century that Eastern Europe—particularly Poland and Russia— began to contribute. Whatever genetic explanations come to mind, the delayed appearance of mathematical genius in Eastern Europe indicates that an enormous amount of "talent" was wasted prior to the nineteenth century.

To these studies, let us add a piquant hint of what might be one of the more perverse investigations of our times, could it be fully conducted. On October 16, 1957, shortly after the prideful announcement of the launching of Sputnik I, *Pravda* published a list of the thirty-four Soviet "heroes of Science" to whom the chief credit was due for this world-shaking achievement. The list was reprinted in the

TABLE I. *Thirty-Seven Mathematicians Classified According to Father's Occupational Class*

Occupational Class	Name	Number	Percent	Estimated Percentage Distribution of Male Labor Force
I. Aristocrats and professional, technical workers, etc.	Descartes, Hermite, Pascal, Cauchy, Cayley, Galois, Hamilton, Lobachevski, Abel, Euler, Kummer, Poincaré, Riemann, 8 members of Bernoulli family, Dedekind, Leibniz, Weierstrass	24	65	1
II. Directors, officials, proprietors	Boole, Fermat, Jacobi, Kovalevski, Kronecker, Sylvester, Lagrange	7	19	2
III. Farm owners, managers	Newton	1	3	5
IV. Sales workers	———	0	0	1
V. Clerical workers, etc.		0	0	5
VI. Craftsmen, foremen, etc.	Gauss, Monge, Fourier *	3	8	5
VII. Operatives, etc.	———	0	0	1
VIII. Service workers		0	0	5
IX. Farm laborers	Laplace, † Zeno of Elea ‡	2	5	60
X. Other laborers	———	0	0	15
Totals		37	100	100

* Fourier, the son of a tailor, was adopted by a wealthy woman when he was eight years old.
† Laplace was reared in a religious orphanage.
‡ Zeno is reported to have been a "self-taught country boy"; after 2,000 years, his family status is understandably vague!

New York *Times* on the following day. It must be admitted that research into the social origins of these men is extremely difficult; the Russian system is not one where either pride in social or biological descent is fashionable. Yet, from the *Soviet Encyclopaedia*, and Western sources, one finds out enough about this select list to justify the suspicion that its social origins are precisely those of the British Men of Science described by Galton in 1865, and of the American scientists studied by Cattell five decades ago.

Most of these men were born long enough before the October Revolution of 1917 so that their academic careers were fixed well before the Revolution, and certainly before the Soviet educational system began to take its present form in the early 1930s. Kapitsa, perhaps the most important, is the son of a general in the Engineering Corps of the Czarist army, and was educated in the aristocratic polytechnic school at Kronstadt, at the Petersburg Polytechnic, and at Cambridge. Lavrentyev, mathematician, described socially as the "son of a scientific worker," is in fact the son of a professor of mechanics at the University of Moscow. M. A. Leontovich, physicist, is the son of A. V. Leontovich, late head of the Department of Normal Physiology at Kiev. V. G. Khlopin, whose contributions to optics are noteworthy, carried on his first scientific activities in the laboratory of his father, G. V. Khlopin, a professor of physics at the University of Moscow. Another great name in optics is that of A. A. Lebedev, son of Professor P. N. Lebedev, also lately of the University of Moscow. B. A. Kazansky, chemist, is also the "son of a scientific worker."

In short, the "heroes of Soviet Science," at least to a most recent date, are likely to be, in the first instance, the products of a Czarist education; they come from precisely that "professional, technical, and kindred workers" class from which the great mathematicians of the Western world, the British and American scientists, and the scholarship winners of the National Merit Scholarship competitions come. The Russians are acutely conscious of the problem; the new dispensation in education announced by Khrushchev in the fall of 1958 is an example. The device of requiring students to intersperse their university and technical studies with labor among the masses was admittedly to be instituted because of the growing estrangement of the intellectuals—presumably, now, "scientific workers"—from the proletariat. Mr. Khrushchev has himself revealed a sensitivity to the problem during his recent American tour; he told his September 16th dinner audience that the schism hoped for by the enemies of the Communist system would not in fact take place.

Despite Mr. Khrushchev's disclaimers, and since there is no Soviet social science that would enable us to know the facts, one can only suspect that in this problem Soviet communism, like American democracy, faces its greatest challenge to the survival of an equalitarian credo. If the high abilities of mathematicians and physicists are genetic, the dream of absolute equalitarianism to come must vanish, as the dream of "All men are created equal" has been tarnished in our country. On the contrary, there is much reason to believe that even in Soviet Russia today, high ability has been transmitted by a social milieu at least as powerful as the influence of the genes.

It will be recalled that Peter the Great, seeking to westernize Russia, imported numbers of German and other scholars; and that Catherine the Great followed Peter in giving especial attention to the Academy and the University of Moscow. The academic immigrants to Russia stipulated as one condition of their accepting employment the establishment of good schools for their own children, to be connected with the higher institutions where they labored, and to be supervised by them. In the remarkable reappearance in successive generations of notable scientists in the same family, that was paralleled in many Western families but nowhere to the same degree as in Russian institutions, the strength of societal influences even stronger than biological inheritance may be glimpsed.

The Prevalence of "Talent"

As suggested earlier, studies of demonstrated ability in the United States point to the same class pattern characteristic of the European past and present. Investigations by Schneider and by Cattell show a heavy concentration of American scientists derived from the upper middle classes. There were also, said Cattell, qualitative as well as quantitative differences: "A larger proportion of the scientists born on farms were of low distinction and a small proportion of higher distinction. However, no home of a person engaged in domestic service or in day labor even of the highest grades produced an eminent scientist."

Every study employing tests on a national scale has shown the coincidence of the "talented" with social and occupational class, geographic regions, and ethnic and national origin. Among these endeavors, all in a manner devices for "talent searching," have been Army Alpha of World War I, the Army GCT of World War II, and the current National Merit Scholarship competitions. One would judge, from the findings of these endeavors, that "talent" is to be found most frequently among descendants of the North European stocks (excepting, only, the "pure" English and Scotch-descended Southern mountaineers) than among South Europeans and Negroes; among urban and suburban dwellers than in the country; and among Protestants (excepting, again, those of the South) and Jews than among Catholics.

The results of the National Merit Scholarship selections for 1956 are particularly useful for enabling one to estimate how many "talented" youngsters there are in the United States, for finding out the social and economic classes from which they come, and for estimating how much "talent" is being wasted.

To make such an estimate, let us assume the convenient "upper 2 percent" formula so frequently taken as the boundary within which our highest potential is found. In itself, this sharp delimitation is an unconscious revelation of the genetic obsession. James Bryant Conant, among others, has notably expanded the borders so far as to include the "upper 30 percent". For our purposes, let us meet the problem at its severest limits by assuming that the "talented" are limited to the upper 2 percent of high-school graduates.

In 1959 the number of high-school graduates was 1,400,-000. Using the upper 2 percent rate, 28,000 of these were "talented" youngsters. For various reasons—perhaps genetic, perhaps environmental—on examination we find, by extension of the National Merit data, that the 28,000 residual "talented"—the upper 2 percent—are concentrated in the upper social and economic classes of the population. We owe to the National Merit Scholarship competitions a fairly precise demonstration of this fact, set forth in Table II.

How much "talent" are we wasting?

The answer, of course, will depend on how strong is one's belief in the genetic nature of "talent." If one agrees with Sir Francis Galton, or Pitirim Sorokin, the answer would be: "Very little!" This school of thought would hold that the existence of "natural" ability is reflected in the National Merit Scholarship findings, as it is in Galton's studies of British Men of Science, and in the other numerous studies of "genius" quoted earlier.

On the other hand, a confirmed environmentalist might argue that the vast majority of children, granted superior environment and education, are potential candidates for the ranks of the "talented." We should then be wasting the talents of closer to 2 million children annually: most of the 1,400,000 high-school graduates, plus many of their approximately 900,000 fellow students who do not graduate from high school.

Forsaking this extreme, it may appear reasonable to believe that the potential of "talent" in the American population is better suggested, not by the 54 "talented" children

TABLE II. *Distribution of "Talented" Children by Occupational Class of Fathers*

Occupational Class	Percentage Distribution of Male Labor Force *	Talented Children Number	Percent
I. Professional, technical workers etc.	8.5	12,649	45.2
II. Managers, officials, and proprietors	12.2	6,216	22.2
III. Sales workers	5.6	1,838	6.6
IV. Clerical workers, etc.	6.5	1,514	5.4
V. Craftsmen, foremen, etc.	19.1	3,027	10.8
VI. Operatives, etc.	21.4	1,459	5.2
VII. Service workers †	6.4	378	1.3
VIII. Farmers, farm managers, farm laborers, and foremen †	11.8	865	3.1
IX. Laborers, except farm and mine	8.5	54	.2
Totals	100.0	28,000	100.0

* In 1956, the same year as the scholarship data.

† This list of nine basic occupational classes is derived from the census list of eleven. For lack of precise data in the National Merit Scholarship Reports, we have been obliged to combine in "Service workers" the two separate census classifications, "Private household workers" and "Service workers except private"; and into Class VIII of "Farmers, etc.," "Farmers and farm managers," and "Farm laborers and foremen." The "Service workers" class combination does not greatly affect the results; however, if "Farmers and farm managers" could be separated from "Farm laborers and foremen," "Farmers (owners) and farm managers" would then be shown to have a much higher productive ratio, while "farm laborers and foremen" would fall at, or very near, the bottom of the list.

of laborers, but by the 12,649 "talented" children of professional, technical, and kindred workers. If we assume that the nation's children are distributed, by occupation of father, in the same proportions as the occupational distribution of the male labor force, then our estimates show that 1 out of every 3,600 children of the laboring classes is classified as a "talented" person; while 1 in every 15 children of the professionals will earn that title. Those who believe that 3,900,000 male lawyers, college professors, physicians, and other professionals, and an equal number of laborers, as tallied by the United States Census in 1956, were cast in their respective roles because of their genes, will also believe in the continued persistence of a biologically hereditary class of "talented" persons.

In this essay we may be permitted to take a leaf from the book of the students of population, and develop a range of estimates, under the severe limitation of an "upper 2 percent" for the "talented," of the potential number of such children in this country. But note that the "2 percent" limitation is arbitrary and if we admit that educational and other environmental influences can enlarge the ability scope of the child the boundaries of the potential talent pool must be widened. If we believe that heredity is all that matters, the number of the "talented" (currently 28,000) will total 2 percent of each year-class, and we must reconcile ourselves to the fact that about 45 percent of this number—12,649— will come from the most-favored occupational classes in our population. Each of the other occupational classes will, under this theory, have the same ratio of the 28,000 total developed earlier, and we can visualize few, if any, "wasted talents." This becomes our low estimate.

In our medium and high estimates, we keep constant the number of "talented" (12,649) to be derived from the highest class—the professionals; this can serve as the standard to which children of other occupational groups might conform. In our highest estimate-level, every occupational class is producing "talented" youngsters in the same proportion as the professionals: or, in a ratio of 1 "talented" child to every 15 children in the year-class population. Our medium estimates are arbitrarily set at half of the high.

TABLE III. *Range of Estimated Numbers of "Talented" Children by Occupational Class of Fathers*

Occupational Class	Low Estimate	Medium Estimate	High Estimate
I. Professional, technical workers, etc. (standard)	12,649	12,649	12,649
II. Managers, officials, and proprietors	6,216	9,077	18,155
III. Sales workers	1,838	4,167	8,333
IV. Clerical workers, etc.	1,514	4,836	9,673
V. Craftsmen, foremen, etc.	3,027	14,212	28,423
VI. Operatives, etc.	1,459	15,922	31,845
VII. Service workers	378	4,762	9,524
VIII. Farmers, farm managers, farm laborers, and foremen	865	8,780	17,560
IX. Laborers, except farm and mine	54	6,325	12,649
Totals	28,000	80,730	148,811

In brief: our argument is that, could we but give to every child in the land the same opportunities for intellectual stimulation now enjoyed by the children of professional, technical, and kindred workers, we could increase our "talent pool" fivefold. Even if we could move but part-way in this direction, as suggested by our medium estimate, we could have available more than 80,000 "talents" in place of our presently estimated 28,000. The measure of future potential would be even greater; for the elevation of the entire community would inevitably raise the standard, by increasing the proportion of "talented" to be derived from the top class.

As far short as we are of realizing the goal of equal opportunity in our public schools, there are few who would argue against the possibility of at least doubling our present potential of very able persons. Judgments about the academic ability now being produced by different classes and groups, and estimates as to their potential, assume a degree of equality of opportunity far greater than presently exists, in family, in community, in school.

On the floor of Congress, in 1837, the dedicated spokesman for states' rights, John C. Calhoun, argued for the continued enslavement of the Negro on the basis of his inherent racial inability to attain to the higher mental processes. He declared himself willing to grant the intellectual capacity of the race when he found a Negro who could parse a Greek sentence, or do an exercise in higher mathematics. The great South Carolinian was misinformed, even in his own generation, for these high tests of capacity invoked by Calhoun had already then been surpassed by Africans and American Negroes in European and American universities.

This writer is presently conducting a study of American Negroes holding the academic doctorate, with the aim of determining, if possible, the central factors involved in the emergence of unusual academic ability in this minority population. Although the study is far from completion, preliminary findings suggest an enormous untapped potential in this population—one whose representatives now infrequently qualify for National Merit Scholarships. Similarly, few if any white children native to the Southern Appalachians qualify for these grants, and, genetically, this latter population, composed principally of what Berea's late President Frost called "our contemporary Elizabethans," must be acknowledged to be the "purest Anglo-Saxon stock" in the United States.

The sample for this study, which is limited to Negroes who have achieved the doctorate, shows, among other features, one fascinating ancestral fact. When the birthplaces of parents and grandparents are "spotted" on a county map of the United States, a pattern of concentration appears. Among the counties showing a high concentration of ancestors are: Dinwiddie county, Virginia; Richland county, South Carolina; Madison county, Kentucky; and, most prolific of all, Perry county, in Alabama.

One searches in vain for any factors that would differentiate these particular counties from dozens of others among the South's 1,200 counties—that is, until one lays the map

showing the birthplaces of the grandparents of Negroes who
have won the highest American academic degree over a map
published by Thomas Jesse Jones in 1915, as a part of a
study of Negro education sponsored by the Phelps-Stokes
Fund and the United States Office of Education. The Jones'
map shows the location of every school offering education
on the secondary school level for Negroes in the South at
that time; they were principally privately controlled and
supported institutions, as even so recently there existed few
publicly supported secondary schools for Negroes in the
South.

In the text accompanying the maps, Jones had given
meticulous histories of their service, and estimates of their
worth at the time of his inspections. Reading the text, examining the two maps, one begins to suspect that there is
more than a coincidental relationship between them. Most
of these mission schools were founded immediately after
the Civil War; they had been the joyous recourse of most
of the grandparents of these contemporary academic doctors.

The inspection tells one that Dinwiddie county, Virginia,
was the location of the Dinwiddie County Training School,
a mission-founded private school in the 1870s, that shortly
before its inspection in 1916 had begun to receive state support. One of its first Negro principals was James Colson, a
graduate, Phi Beta Kappa, of Dartmouth College. Also located in the county, in its seat at Petersburg, was the Virginia Normal and Industrial Institute (now, the Virginia
State College), staffed from its inception in 1882 by the best
trained Negro personnel available in the nation.

Madison county, Kentucky, is the seat of Berea College; this college, founded by the redoubtable Kentucky-bred abolitionist, John G. Fee, admitted Negroes freely to all of its grades, from elementary school through college, until the United States Supreme Court, in 1907, upheld the segregating Kentucky Day Law of 1904.

In Columbia, in Richland county, South Carolina, were Benedict College and Allen University, two institutions that liberally scattered their graduates throughout the surrounding countryside, to teach in the log cabins and shacks that passed for schools so long a time ago, but with a devotion beyond present imagining.

And Perry county, Alabama, was the seat, at Marion, of the Lincoln Normal School—to very recent years a Yankee-staffed grade and high school that was founded immediately after the Civil War. Viewing on this map the bare spaces in the surrounding "black belt" counties of Alabama, where the percentage of Negro illiteracy, of farm tenancy, and of other indices of deprivation, scarcely varies from those ratios in Perry county, the viewer can scarcely doubt that the very superior educational institution that was the Lincoln Normal School accounts for much of the difference. Undeniably, Negro "talent" of highest quality has had its ancestral roots in Perry county, which has given us a federal judge, distinguished physicians, as well as research scientists and other scholars with doctoral degrees from America's great universities.

Was there a particular variety of intellectual Negro genes in Perry county? I think it unlikely.

More likely, I think it, that the happiest of circumstances conspired in Perry county to contribute "talent" to America —the circumstance of a first-class school, even for plantation ex-slaves. By this and other tokens, I take it that in every depressed racial group, in every "lower class" occupational group in the country, in every culturally deprived geographical region, there are today potentially "talented" youngsters of every economic or racial or religious persuasion. Indeed, the surface has scarcely been tapped.

The specifics of saving this now-wasted talent are scarcely within the scope of this paper. Clearly, it involves an enterprise more heroic—and costly—than that of providing subsidies for ten or twenty or even a hundred thousand individual youngsters.

The waste calls for the improvement of education in the large for every child in America; for the children of 4 million laborers, of more than 4.5 million farmers and farm laborers, of 9 million operatives, among a present total of some 48,000,000 male workers in the land. Beyond the schools are the other improvements in the level of life to which this nation is already committed; for that relatively brief historical moment through which the nation's destiny now passes, the school must remain our last, best hope, for the utilization of the highest capacities of all of our people to the full, and for the elimination of waste of high human ability.

EDUCATION AND EMPLOYMENT

by SEYMOUR L. WOLFBEIN

ON THE masthead of a major journal in the field of vocational guidance there appeared for a long time the following inscription: "Vocational guidance is the process of assisting the individual to choose an occupation, prepare for it, enter upon, and progress in it."

To those who are now attempting to assess the problems and opportunities of the 1960s, this maxim must have a nostalgic ring indeed. It conjures up a rather neatly packaged world where goals may be firmly and early set, pathways to those goals clearly defined, and where, in spite of life's many pitfalls the established pathways can be followed to their expected ends, with the proper help from properly trained professional personnel.

Not so in the 1960s—just as it had not been so for many decades before.

Education and guidance seek to relate and orient the individual child and youth to the forces of his environment—and one of the major forces involved is that of work. And

Seymour L. Wolfbein is Deputy Assistant Secretary of Labor, Washington, D.C.

one of the major features of the world of work is *change*. The goal of education and guidance in this regard might therefore be more aptly put: To help the individual withstand the onslaughts and, in fact, take advantage of the inevitable changes which will take place in the world of work.

These two conceptions of the orientation process of young people to their economic environment are meaningfully different in a number of important respects. At the very least, they create different expectations for the educational system itself (how and what to teach and guide), which is now engaged in a major reevaluation of methods and goals; and for the young person himself, who must view the occupational world not as a great array of fixed job slots with ready accommodations for those with different talents, aptitudes, and interests, but as a constantly changing structure with a constantly changing set of educational and training prerequisites and functions and responsibilities.

It is against this background of change in the work world and the significant emphasis it gives to the need for flexibility on the part of education and training, educators and trainers, and the educated and trained that this brief essay discusses some of the major dimensions of our manpower future.

Youth in the Work Force of the 1960s

According to most recent Labor Department estimates, we can expect the American labor force to increase from about 73.5 million persons in 1960 to about 87 million persons in

1970. Because of the historically almost unique kind of population changes we will experience during this decade, young people will play a critically important role in the 13.5 million or almost 20 percent increase in the number of workers during the 1960s. These changes are detailed in Table I.

TABLE I. *Expected Labor Force Changes*
By Age and Sex: 1960–1970

	In the Labor Force		Change: 1960–70	
	In 1960	In 1970	Number	Percent
	(in millions)		(in millions)	
All persons 14 years and older	73,550	87,092	13,542	18.4
Males	49,971	57,443	7,472	15.0
14–24	8,963	13,121	4,158	46.4
25–34	10,913	12,173	1,260	11.5
35–44	11,367	10,999	−368	−3.2
45–54	9,681	10,725	1,044	10.8
55–64	6,484	7,721	1,237	19.1
65 and over	2,563	2,704	141	5.5
Females	23,579	29,649	6,070	25.7
14–24	4,822	7,046	2,224	46.1
25–34	4,364	4,905	541	12.4
35–44	5,268	5,470	202	3.8
45–54	5,141	6,555	1,414	27.5
55–64	3,031	4,313	1,282	42.3
65 and over	953	1,360	407	42.7

Source: U.S. Department of Labor, Bureau of Labor Statistics

There are at least three major points which this kind of labor force change underscores in terms of the role of youth.

In the first place, the sheer numbers of young people participating as economically active members of the population will reach an historic high. In total, a little over 20 million persons fourteen to twenty-four years of age will be in the labor force in 1970—an increase of almost 6.5 million over 1960.

This is the age cohort, of course, which was born in the high birth rate years of the immediate postwar decade 1946 through 1956 and who will reach labor force age (by definition age fourteen) during the 1960s. The numbers of workers in this age group in 1970 will be only a little short of the total number of people in that age group in 1930. It will be two and a half times as large as at the turn of this century, 60 percent higher than at the middle of this century.

Second, the relative increase in these young workers will be just as significant. The rate of increase among young male workers during the 1960s will be five times as large as the corresponding rate among male workers of all other ages; the rate of increase among young female workers during the same period of time will be more than double the corresponding rate among female workers of all other ages. As a result, the proportion of the total labor force made up of youth (fourteen to twenty-four years of age) will rise to the point where they will account for almost one out of every four workers in the United States in 1970.

Since the beginning of this century, the proportion of the working population made up of persons in the younger age groups has declined steadily because of the significant and substantial drop in labor market participation among youth. This trend, in turn has been due to a wide variety of factors, among which legislation and regulations concerning youth employment and increased school enrollments were most important. This long-term trend is now being reversed, despite the expected continuation of the decline in labor market participation rates among the young. Again, the sheer volume of young persons coming into the labor force will raise the proportion they make up of the total work force throughout the decade of the '6os.

The strategic role of the younger person in the labor force of the '6os receives additional emphasis, in the third place, when viewed against the trends for other groups in the working population. The following brief summary makes the point:

The labor force increase of 13.5 million during the 1960s will come from the following groups:

Age	Percent
14–24	47
25–34	13
35–44	−1
45–64	37
65 and over	4
Total	100

Thus, just about one out of every two new additions to the labor supply in the '6os will come from the younger age groups. In fact the two groups most often dubbed as "problems"—the younger and older—will account for the preponderant majority of our additional workers during the decade. The key part these persons will have in the labor force of the immediate future is underscored by the fact that, in the face of increases practically across the board, the prime working age group thirty-five to forty-four years old will actually decline by 1970, as the low-birth depression years of the 1930s continue to affect our population and manpower posture.

There are many other significant aspects of overall manpower change during the '60s which the reader may want to see by examining Table 1. One in particular may be mentioned at this point. It will be noted that a little over 6 million, or 45 percent, of the total labor force increase of this decade will be made up of women. More than 1 out of every 3 in this 6 million increase will be accounted for by the young women fourteen to twenty-four, whose relative rise over the decade will exactly match the increase among the males in the same young age cohort. The number of young women in the work force in 1970 will be triple the number at the beginning of this century, about 50 percent higher than at the middle of this century.

Thus, the numbers and proportions of younger workers—both male and female—are going to reach historic levels, emphasized all the more by the accompanying differential trends among the rest of the age groups in the working population.

Industrial and Occupational Change

A recent New York *Times* advertisement by a long established multibranch company calls for applications from persons with experience in:

Transistorized circuitry	Ferret Reconnaissance
Inertial guidance—missiles	Human factors science

Gyrodynamics-supersonic aircraft	Micro-miniaturization
Shielding design-atomic power	Data telemetry

This "help wanted ad" contains occupations which were hardly even known just a few years ago. Dealing as they do with some of the frontiers of current work in the physical sciences they are representative of the great forces of change in the world of work. How many persons are there in the United States today who carefully chose, prepared for, and entered these occupations?

This brief listing of occupations is also symptomatic of a basic and overridingly important shift in the very industrial and occupational structure of the United States—a shift which took place slowly but almost inexorably throughout this century, reached an historic turning point during the '50s and will continue to be a major force to be reckoned with during the '60s.

In a recent month during 1959, persons who work for a wage or salary (but including farmers as well as farm hands) were distributed as follows among the major industries of the United States:

(in millions)

Manufacturing	16.1	Transportation and public	3.9
Construction	2.8	utilities	
Mining	.7	Trade	11.2
Agriculture	6.4	Finance, insurance	2.4
		Service	6.6
		Government	8.2
	26.0		32.3

On the left we have the workers who produce "goods": all of the items literally manufactured—autos, steel, rubber, apparel, furniture, chemicals, etc.; everything built—the millions of homes every year, bridges, highways, factories, office buildings, etc.; everything mined from the ground—coal, lead, zinc, gold, uranium, etc.; all the food, feed and fiber produced by the agricultural sector of the American economy.

On the right we have the workers who produce "services" —who buy and sell, finance and service, teach, work for the government as firemen, policemen, economists or clerks, etc., etc. They now outnumber the "goods" producers by 6 millions. Had we, in addition to the wage and salary workers, included persons earning their livelihood by owning their own business off the farm, the difference would have been even much greater in favor of the service sector, since most self-employed persons are in such sectors as trade.

Throughout this century, workers in the service producing industries have been gaining on those producing goods; they overtook them in the early part of the '50s, have moved steadily ahead since then, and there is nothing in the offing which will change this trend as we move into the '60s.

Inevitably, this kind of change in industrial structure has brought a corresponding change in the occupations we follow as workers. Here again is a brief recapitulation of past, present, and expected future developments:

	1910	1959	1970
	(in percent)		
All workers	100	100	100
White-collar	22	42	45
Professional and technical	5	11	13
Proprietary and managerial	7	11	11
Clerical and sales	10	20	21

Blue-collar	37	37	36
Skilled	12	13	13
Semiskilled	14	18	18
Unskilled	11	6	5
Service	10	12	13
Farm	31	9	6

In a real way this brief table reflects some of the major social and economic changes of the twentieth century in this country:

1. The almost complete turn-around from a rural to urban economy: in 1910 almost one out of every three workers was on the farm; today the ratio is below one in ten and still going down.

2. The emergence to a majority position of the white-collar group in the late 1950s: in 1910, more than one in three employed persons was a blue-collar worker and only about one in five a white-collar worker; now the white-collar worker outnumbers his blue-collar counterpart and is scheduled to increase his numerical and proportionate advantage during the '60s.

3. The great growth in the professional and clerical and sales groups, which have doubled their standings in the occupational hierarchy over the past fifty odd years.

4. The stable (but key) position of the skilled craftsman.

5. And the enormous decline in unskilled jobs in the United States.

As can be seen from the summary figures, these occupational trends are expected to continue into the '60s, highlighted particularly by the persistent growth in white-collar jobs. This growth, it may be added, is expected to affect the goods-producing as well as the service-producing sectors of the economy, as indeed it already has.

For example: In 1948 there were among manufacturing (factory) employees a little short of 13 million production workers and about 2.5 million nonproduction workers. The former represent workers in and around the factory production line; the latter include largely the clerical, managerial, and professional personnel in the offices of factory plants. Ten years later (1958) production workers had fallen by a million under the impact of the business downturn of that year; nonproduction workers had increased by 1.25 million over the same period of time.

These expected trends should not be taken to denigrate the continued importance of at least one major group among the blue-collar workers—the skilled craftsmen, for whom the demand is expected to be substantial in the decade to come. The situation in this field, in fact, illustrates one of the points we are coming to in the following section—the role of training.

For example: The U.S. Bureau of Apprenticeship reports that the number of new building trades craftsmen emerging from apprenticeship training programs between 1950 and 1958 was less than the number of journeymen lost to the trade because of death and retirement.

All in all, then, the '60s are expected to witness a significant increase in the skill level of the labor force across the occupational structure.

Some Implications

It is when we juxtapose the findings of the two preceding substantive sections that some of the major issues of the '60s with regard to employment of youth come into focus. The conjunction of the size and composition of labor force growth and the kind of industrial and occupational changes we have described so far poses some of the major problems —as well as opportunities—of the coming ten years.

On the one hand, the expectations are for a significant increase in the number and proportion of jobs demanding increased education and training in both the white-collar and blue-collar occupations. On the other hand, the preponderant increase in available manpower will come from the young, some of whom will still be in the process of obtaining their education and training, practically all of whom will be at the beginnings of their career development. In the age group from which we normally draw a substantial proportion of our higher level personnel, we face a deficit of experienced workers.

Thus once again is underscored the truth of the axiom "what is past is prologue" in the field we are discussing. The very low birth rates of the '30s, succeeded by the huge upturn in births in the '40s have given us a unique configuration in our population and manpower distribution. When related to the kind of industrial and occupational changes we can expect, we can at least anticipate the uneven kind of problem posed by the necessity to provide employment opportunities for a substantially increased number of young men and women, while engaged in the task of filling an increasing number of professional, technical, and skilled jobs in the face of a shortage in one of the prime working-age groups.

In a free and democratic society the pathways available for meeting such a set of problems are essentially twofold: the provision of the best kind of education and guidance to all, consonant with the principle of free choice and based on the individual's talents, interests, and aptitudes; and the best kinds of selection, utilization, and organizational procedures on the part of employers, be they government, industry, or business.

All of this, of course, can take place only in the context of continued economic growth with high levels of employment. All of the estimates and projections, as well as reflections, presented here are predicated on a continuation of the kind of economic growth we have had since the end of World War II. Granting these assumptions, there are at least five points that may be made briefly concerning the relationships between education and employment:

1. As we already have indicated, education and training represent the major catalyst for bringing together and meshing the occupational demands of the future with the resources available to meet them. This, of course, is one of the traditional jobs of education; it may be more difficult, it certainly will be much more extensive in the decade ahead. The discussions by John Gardner and Ralph Tyler in these volumes point up some of the perspectives and issues in this field.

2. The impact of the labor market upon education in the '60s will be highlighted by higher educational and training prerequisites for employment. The almost perfect match between level of educational attainment and the growth areas of the occupational structure can be seen from the following brief summary of the amount of schooling by members of different occupational groupings.

Occupation	Average Years of School Completed
White-Collar	
Professional and technical	16+
Clerical	12.5
Proprietary and managerial	12.4
Sales	12.4
Blue-Collar	
Skilled	10.5
Semiskilled	9.5
Unskilled	8.5
Service	9.6
Farmers	8.6
Farm Workers	8.2

Thus, it is the occupations which require higher educational attainment that represent the growth areas of the future. And, even in these occupations the educational requirements continue to rise. Witness the increasing time required for an engineering degree; the recent increase from four to five years for a baccalaureate in pharmacy and architecture; the increasing demand for teachers with master's degrees, the rising demand for secretaries and clerical personnel with some post high-school work, etc.

3. At the same time, there is every indication that young people in ever-increasing numbers and proportions will be going after the increased education and training which our changing job structure will apparently call for. Back in 1940, only 26 percent of the population fifteen years of age and over were high-school graduates; the Census Bureau projects a figure of 45 percent for 1970. Similarly, only 3.8 million in our population twenty years of age and over were college graduates in 1940; the Census projects a tripling of that figure for 1970.

4. The education—occupation—employment links which we have emphasized so much in this discussion have and will prove themselves out in the acid test of the labor market. One of the more persevering labor force trends in this country is the inverse relationship between educational attainment and occupational status on the one hand and the rate of unemployment on the other. Here was the situation in the spring of 1959; the numbers may change with alterations in the business cycle, but the relationships among the different occupational groups stay on:

Occupational Level	*Rate of Unemployment* *(in percent)*
Unskilled	11.8
Semiskilled	7.5
Skilled	5.4
Sales	4.1
Clerical	3.3
Proprietors, managerial	1.4
Professional and technical	1.3

5. The various changes described so far emphasize once again a long standing problem which fits squarely within

the context of our discussion on the relationship between education and employment—the school dropout. Studied extensively for many years by both public and private groups, the young person who ends his educational career before high-school graduation still represents one of the more intractable problems.

According to recent investigations about 1 out of every 3 dropouts from the school system leaves during the eighth grade or before; 2 out of 3 never get to senior high school, i.e., they drop out before the tenth grade. Thus, a huge proportion of these persons not only do not get the high-school education which is becoming a minimum requirement for more and more jobs; they leave before those grades in which most kinds of formal guidance and occupational information programs begin to take place.

In terms of labor market adjustment, the dropouts do very poorly indeed. For example, a study of the contrasting experience between girl dropouts and girl high-school graduates who did not go on to college showed that two out of every three of the graduates obtained jobs in the white-collar clerical fields, while two-thirds of the dropouts found jobs in the unskilled ranks as waitresses, etc. But by far the sharpest difference among both boys and girls (dropouts vs. high school graduates not going on to college) was in the unemployment they experienced. On all scores—in terms of rates of unemployment, spells of unemployment, and total time since leaving school spent as unemployed workers, the dropouts had a much worse record than the graduates.

The changing labor force, industrial, and occupational pictures for the 1960s with their emphasis on stiffer competition at higher skill levels and higher skill development make the prognosis for these young persons even more negative. Others in these volumes discuss the quantitative and qualitative dimensions of the problems in education for the '60s. At this point, however, two relevant matters warrant consideration.

The first is the necessity—since a large proportion of dropouts are retarded in the early grades and actually leave well before the completion of high school—to consider the development of programs of guidance and counseling at the elementary school level. The second relates to the possibility of increasing the "holding power" of the schools through the design of courses of instruction which can both hold the interest of and be of substantive value to some of the young people who do not make any progress within existing curricula. Is it possible to offer earlier a broader choice of educational avenues along which this kind of student can move with profit and dignity?

Conclusions

We have alluded to the kinds of expectations which will be generated by the changing manpower picture of the 1960s. We conclude with a somewhat closer and more concrete indication of what some of these expectations are likely to be—for the three broad areas which together are going to make the difference in how successfully we manage our affairs during the decade.

As to the educational process itself and those who will be responsible for its operation and sense of direction, perhaps

the best way to underline again the overriding importance
of this sector to our manpower future is as follows: we have
indicated that about 20 million persons fourteen to twenty-
four years of age will be in the American labor force in 1970.
Simple arithmetic shows that this group is now (1960) four
to fourteen years of age—it is, or will shortly be, the elementary school population of the United States, which will
move through the grades, through secondary school and
college as the decade advances. In other words, just about
all of the 20 millions of young people who are going to be
such an important part of the work force are right now
within the purview of our educational and training institutions. What we do and plan to do right now will have a
really determining effect on the knowledge and skills, the
arts and sciences, the attitudes and motivations toward work
with which this critical part of our manpower is endowed.

This, perhaps, is at the core of what we expect from education in its relationship to employment—in concert, of
course, with the other responsible agents in this field, i.e.,
the parents and other community organizations.

For education, the expectations include some major problems of a quantitative and qualitative dimension. Not only
will the numbers with whom the educational institutions
have to cope increase, but so will the demand for quality of
curriculum geared to the higher training and skill development requirements of the world of work of the '60s. These
considerations underscore, at the same time, the critical importance of guidance and counseling of young people in their
career planning as part of the educational process.

Advances in education and training are, or course, by no means the entire answer to our manpower problems. They can never, by themselves, guarantee successful performance and utilization of the labor force. Side by side with an adequate preparation of the new labor supply has to come some very careful manpower planning on the part of employing institutions themselves.

We did not have to call upon the talents of a prophet or seer to anticipate some of the critical manpower problems of the '60s—the tremendous inflow of younger workers seeking their first job, the emerging shortage group in the ages thirty-five to forty-four years, etc. In very much the same way organizations, for example, can obtain a substantial amount of information concerning their manpower problems by a simple replacement schedule indicating the exits from their labor force to be expected simply on the basis of retirements to come—and set themselves up to meet the needs these exits will inevitably generate.

This is why the role of organizational and managerial policy—not only in terms of selection, training, utilization and setting standards of work but in careful and creative manpower planning—is so important. In fact, it is a most necessary complement to the points we raised on education and training. We call upon the educational system and the student for a maximum effort and investment in training and skill development. We should follow up with the maximum effort and investment in looking ahead in the manpower field by employers as well.

As in the arena of education, much is still left to be discovered in the field of organizational programs and planning. We close this part of our discussion with the following quotation from the significant work on *The Ineffective Soldier* by Eli Ginzberg and his associates which is very much to this point:

Much is known about the way in which these several approaches can contribute to effective performance, but much remains to be learned. For instance, the proper balancing of the rate of technological improvement with additional efforts to raise the skill level of those who must manage, operate, and maintain the increasingly complex structures warrants further study. So too does the problem of work motivation. We are only at the beginning of understanding the marked differences between the strongly and poorly motivated in the world of work. We also need new knowledge about how the individual, his immediate work group, and the larger organization can be more effectively integrated so that performance can be improved.[1]

These then, are some of the expectations from management in relation to the manpower future of the '60s.

Finally, we come to the youth themselves.

Their expectations also have both a quantitative and qualitative dimension. With regard to their role as workers they will find, first, more competition simply because of the numbers of their colleagues searching for employment. And, as we already have indicated, more and more of their competition will be better and better educated and trained.

Yet, in the face of a significantly changing occupational and industrial structure, they will have a major advantage, in view of the expected deficit in the number of their older

---

[1] Eli Ginzberg et al., *Patterns of Performance* (Vol. III of *The Ineffective Soldier*, New York: Columbia University Press, 1959), p. 303.

counterparts, in the competition to fill the higher level jobs. Given a continuation of relatively high levels of economic activity and employment, many may have the opportunity to move ahead in their careers at an accelerated pace.

To achieve these goals youth will have to be adaptable, flexible, and mobile. Every study, incidentally, that has been made shows that mobility varies directly with the amount of education and training a person has—underscoring again the pivotal relationship between education and employment. And this makes sense—after all, the more education and skill an individual has, the better he will be able to respond to new opportunities and new settings in different places and different jobs. This will be all the more important in the '60s when we have to face up to significant changes in our very manpower, industrial, and occupational structure.

THE ARMED SERVICES AS A
TRAINING INSTITUTION

by HAROLD WOOL

DURING the 1950s, military service obligation became an accepted fact of life for young American males approaching adulthood. A post-World War II draft law, enacted in 1948, remained continuously on the statute books throughout the decade and in 1959 was extended by the Congress until 1963. Partly as a result of their military service liability under the law, and partly in voluntary response to the opportunities offered by military careers, over 7 million youths entered active military service. By the end of the decade, fully 70 percent of the men aged twenty-five to twenty-six had entered or completed a tour of active military duty; the remainder consisted almost entirely of those deferred or disqualified for service.

In contrast to earlier periods of full mobilization, when the Armed Services had drawn upon a broad range of adult manpower, the new entrants into military service in recent years

Harold Wool is Staff Director of the Analysis Division, Office of the Assistant Secretary of Defense (Manpower, Personnel, and Reserves).

were mainly in their late teens or early twenties. Relatively few had acquired substantial vocational skills. To most, military service initiated their first departure from home, school, and community. As a result, the Military Establishment which, except in crisis, had been historically relegated to a relatively minor role in the American pattern of life, suddenly emerged as an institution with tremendous significance in the molding of American youth.

An appreciation of the role of the Armed Services as a training and educational institution and as an initial vocational experience for a large segment of our youth requires at the outset some understanding of the nature of the military structure. Military training programs are designed, necessarily, to meet the special needs of the Armed Services for skilled manpower. These needs overlap in some ways, but contrast in other respects, with those of civilian industry. As in the civilian work force, changes in technology have resulted in significant changes in military skill requirements in recent years. These changes, in turn, have had a direct impact on the numbers and kinds of men required for military service and on the nature of military training programs.

In the following sections we shall review, in turn, the military skill structure, major skill trends, changes in the number and characteristics of personnel entering service, the nature and scope of military training programs, and some of the implications of this training for youth in relation to civilian work careers.

The Military Skill Structure

Although some small degree of specialization has always been required of military personnel, the concept of military personnel as "specialists" with widely differing duties, skills, and training is of recent origin. Until a few decades ago, most personnel in our military forces were classified simply as commissioned officers, noncommissioned officers, and privates. The commissioned officers provided the executive and professional leadership; the noncommissioned officers, the direct supervision; and the privates, the mass of combat manpower. As general-duty soldiers or seamen, they also performed a wide range of support duties of an unskilled or semiskilled nature. In those limited instances where more skilled or technical work was required, the lack of occupational specialization and of in-service training systems required resort to special recruitment programs for skilled craftsmen, or to use of auxiliary civilian contract personnel.[1]

This crude military division of labor, although suited to the needs of infantry or cavalry troops in frontier America, proved wholly inadequate to cope with the vastly more complex array of equipment and functions required in our twentieth century military forces, as became painfully evident during the early phases of mobilization in World War

[1] The Navy, we should note, constituted a limited exception to this pattern. The shipboard "rating" structure for enlisted personnel, under which its petty officers are identified in terms of their specialized shipboard duties and skills, traces back to Revolutionary times. These ratings, however, were originally taken over from the civilian merchant fleet, which, until the closing years of the nineteenth century, was also the Navy's principal source of skilled personnel.

I, when shortages of skilled specialists proved to be serious bottlenecks in the organization, equipping, and movement of our troops overseas. It was not until World War II, however, that comprehensive systems for occupational classification of military jobs and personnel were established in each of the Armed Services.

These military occupational classifications have been subject to periodical overhaul since World War II, in response to changing job requirements and training concepts. The number of specialized skills required in each of the Armed Services today provides in itself a striking measure of the wide range and complexity of the military job structure. For enlisted personnel, the number of specialties ranges from about 400 in the Navy and Marine Corps to more than 900 in the Army. These specialties are grouped into a series of occupational ladders, each providing a systematic progression from the entry or apprentice level to journeyman and, finally, to the senior supervisory ranks. Descriptions of these enlisted occupational fields are published by the Armed Services in occupational handbooks for use by counselors, school officials, and individuals interested in Service careers.

A similar pattern of occupational specialization has also emerged for the officer ranks. The pattern of officer-career management, however, is generally designed to provide progressive broadening of professional experience and responsibilities, rather than narrow technical specialization.

The scope and variety of military jobs, and the extent to which they now parallel civilian-type skills, is suggested by the accompanying distribution of enlisted personnel by occupational group. (Table I) These occupational groups are designed generally to match broadly analogous groupings for the civilian labor force, with the obvious exception of "ground combat" skills, which have no civilian counterpart.

TABLE I. *Percentage Distribution of Assigned Enlisted Personnel by Occupational Group, 31 December 1958* *

Group	Percentage of Total Assigned Enlisted Personnel
Total	100.0
Ground combat	12.9
Infantry	6.9
Artillery	3.0
Armored vehicle crews	1.6
Combat engineering	1.4
Electronics	13.5
Electronics equipment maintenance	7.0
Electronics equipment operators, excluding radio	3.2
Radio operators	2.7
Air traffic control	.7
Other technical	7.4
Medical and dental	4.3
Intelligence	1.0
Surveyors and draftsmen	.6
Photography	.5
Weather	.4
Other	.6
Administrative and clerical	20.6
General administration and clerical	6.9
Supply	6.8

Group	Percentage of Total Assigned Enlisted Personnel
Communications	2.4
Personnel	1.7
Disbursing and finance	.8
Machine accounting and statistics	.6
Other	.9
Mechanics and repairmen	25.8
Aircraft and engine, including parts	11.0
Shipboard machinery	4.5
Electrical and wire communications	3.9
Automotive	3.6
Munitions and weapons	2.6
Other	.2
Crafts	7.6
Construction and utilities	3.3
Naval operating crafts	1.3
Metal working	.9
Firefighting	.8
Fabric, rubber, and leather	.5
Other	.7
Services	11.8
Food service	4.7
Security	3.2
Motor transport	2.7
Other	1.2
Miscellaneous (e.g., musicians)	.4

Source: Department of Defense.
* Based on total of approximately 1,890,000 enlisted personnel assigned to units, for whom military occupational specialties were reported. Excludes about 340,000 enlisted personnel not assigned to units, and those with unidentifiable skill, e.g., recruits, trainees, transients, and Navy general duty personnel (seamen, airmen).

This table highlights in a striking way the extent to which the Armed Services now rely on the "soldier-technician." Much has been written about the increased "technicality" of military skills. However, for those whose military service exposure was in World War II or earlier, it may still come as a shock to realize that, for all Services combined, our modern enlisted force now requires twice as many mechanics as it does ground combat specialists; or that the number of electronics equipment maintenance technicians now exceeds the number of infantrymen.

In comparing the military occupational categories with their civilian counterparts, certain unique features of the military job structure should be noted:

First, the very nature of the military mission requires that military personnel be capable of fulfilling a variety of functions, particularly under the stress of combat conditions. Throughout their careers, personnel assigned to specialized tasks may, at the same time, be expected to perform additional duties, such as guard duty or details, commensurate with their rank and supervisory level. This pattern of multiple assignments is particularly characteristic of the Navy job structure where, because of shipboard space limitations, each enlisted man has watch, quarter, and battle station assignments, in addition to strictly technical duties.

Second, unlike the civilian labor force, there is very little provision in the present military occupational structure for the "unskilled laborer" as such. The unskilled and semi-skilled duties of all types, including the "fatigue" details, are in fact mainly performed by junior personnel—recent recruits and trainees—who are, at the same time, serving their apprenticeship or acquiring on-the-job training in a particular military specialty.

Finally, it will be apparent that there is no precise correspondence in job content between the large majority of military and civilian occupations, even though the title may be similar. Many jobs for enlisted men, particularly in the more technical fields, are necessarily more specialized than their civilian counterparts in view of the limited time available for training and utilizing the average recruit. Many other differences in equipment, organization, and function also prevent any precise matching of civilian and military jobs. These are, however, merely an extension of the differences in occupational job content among different civilian industries or even among different employers in the same industry.

Major Skill Trends

The military occupational structure, far from being static, has been in a continuing state of flux and evolution in the post-World War II period. Comparison of the present major occupational groups with those in 1945 and in the early 1950s reveals an unmistakable trend: the sharp relative expansion of the technical-mechanical skill groups at the expense of the more conventional ground combat, crafts, and services occupations. (Table II) The most dramatic increase has been in the electronics group which has more than doubled in relative size since the end of World War II. Over the same period, the percentage of enlisted jobs in ground combat dropped sharply, from nearly 24 percent to less than 13 percent of total strength.

TABLE II. *Percentage Distribution of Enlisted Jobs by Major Occupational Group: End of World War II, During Korean Conflict, and 31 December 1958*

Major Occupational Group	End of World War II	During Korean Conflict	31 Dec. 1958
Electronics	6.2	9.6	13.5
Other technical	6.9	6.9	7.4
Mechanics and repairmen	21.3	22.6	25.8
Administrative and clerical	15.3	20.8	20.6
Crafts and services	26.7	22.7	19.4
Ground combat	23.6	17.4	12.9
Total	100.0	100.0	100.0

Source: *Department of Defense.*

These sharp shifts are traceable in part to fundamental differences in force requirements over the period. The changes in force composition are partially illustrated by the shift in relative strengths among the Services. At the end of World War II, the Army Air Force accounted for 19 percent of total military strength and increased steadily to 33.5 percent, by June, 1959. In contrast, the percentage of active duty strength allocated to the Army dropped sharply from 49 percent at the end of World War II to 34 percent in 1959. These shifts in manpower allocations *among* the military services have been paralleled by equally sharp shifts *within* the Services, with increased emphasis consistently on those branches and elements relying on the newer military technology.

Equally important, and closely related to these shifts in force structure, has been the far-flung impact of the revolution of military technology upon all components of the military services during the past decade. Sustained by a massive research and development effort, and by the many new scientific "break throughs" during and after World War II, the rate of technological advance in military equipment has been unparalleled in our peacetime history. Some of its most sensational impacts have been in the field of electronic equipment, suggested by the fact that the number of electron tubes in the equipment of a Navy destroyer rose from less than 200 in 1940 to as many as 5,400 at present.

The trend towards new and continually more complex equipment is illustrated, too, by the contrast between World War II military aircraft and their recent counterparts. The modern jet bomber includes items of equipment such as speed brakes, cabin pressurization, air conditioning systems, seat ejection, air refueling, anti-fogging, flight control systems, and many others not in existence in World War II bombers. Similar comparisons can readily be made between the World War II submarine and the present nuclear submarine and for a vast array of other military weapons, equipment, and techniques, ranging from atomic artillery to data processing equipment.

The rapid pace of technological advance, in turn, has served to accelerate the long-term trend towards skill specialization. New weapons systems have created the need for completely new types of skills in such fields as guided missiles, rocket propulsion and nuclear weapons assembly. Addition of new and more complex items of equipment in other areas has also resulted in a multiplication of specialized skills in previously established fields, such as radar and aircraft engine maintenance.

The trend has, of course, not been all one-sided. Automation has simplified some operator skills, and stress has been placed upon designing military equipment in a way which will facilitate maintenance. These factors have, however, simply checked what would otherwise have been an even more rapid increase in total technical personnel needs.

Characteristics of Personnel Entering Service

In meeting their formidable requirements for trained specialists, the Armed Services have been confronted by a unique set of conditions, quite unlike those faced by most civilian employers. These stem from the characteristics of the new recruits entering military service in recent years: their youth and lack of working experience, their relatively brief tours of duty, and their heterogeneous backgrounds, interests, and capabilities. Let us review some of these factors briefly.

As shown in Table III, the total number of personnel entering and leaving service each year has gradually declined during the course of the past decade, following the extremely heavy inflow during the Korean conflict. In contrast to these earlier years when heavy reliance was necessarily placed on inductees and on involuntary reserve call-ups, most of the new entrants into military service since 1953 have been voluntary enlistees. With limited exceptions, the Army has been the only Service requiring inductees; and draft calls into that

TABLE III. *Active-Duty Military Strength and Net Gains and Losses* 1951 to 1959 (in thousands)*

Fiscal Year	Strength Beginning of Year	Total Gains	Officer Gains†	Enlisted Gains Total	First Enlistments†	Reserves to Active Duty‡	Inductions	Total Losses
1951	1,460	1,964	138	1,826	630	609	587	175
1952	3,249	1,052	61	991	510	102	379	665
1953	3,636	1,008	47	961	343	54	564	1,089
1954	3,555	685	38	647	329	53	265	938
1955	3,302	730	35	695	440	40	215	1,097
1956	2,935	614	31	583	371	75	137	743
1957	2,806	606	30	576	303	93	180	616
1958	2,796	479	25	454	271	56	127	674
1959	2,601 §	474	22	452	310	31	111	577

Source: Department of Defense.

* Excludes reenlistments in the same Service and intra-Service transfers.

† Includes R.O.T.C. graduates, aviation cadets, Service academy graduates, direct appointments, and various specialized officer procurement programs, as well as Reserve recalls. Reserves accounted for a major portion of officer gains in 1951–52.

‡ Of total enlisted Reservists entering active duty, personnel with prior active service totaled about 430,000 in 1951 and about 30,000 in 1952. Since 1953, over 90 percent have been personnel without prior active service.

§ Preliminary.

Service have dropped substantially, from over 200,000 in 1954 and 1955 to slightly over 100,000 in 1959.

The primary reliance of the Armed Services on voluntary enlistees, has, in turn, directly influenced the age distribution of new personnel. The median age of new enlistees in each year since 1954 has consistently been eighteen and a half years; about 85 percent have been in the age group of seventeen to nineteen years. It thus appears that the large majority of young men have entered military service either immediately after leaving school or after only limited periods of work experience. This, in turn, has compelled the Armed Services to rely very heavily upon in-service training programs to develop their needed skills.

The type and length of skill training programs offered to new entrants into military service have necessarily been influenced by the length of their tours of duty and by the prospects of their retention in service as career personnel. Initial tours of enlisted service in recent years have ranged from two years for inductees to three or four years for regular enlistments. Very few of the inductees—less than 5 percent —continue in the service beyond their obligated two-year tours. The Services, therefore, have relied mainly upon the regular enlistees to meet their requirements for career noncommissioned officers and skilled technicians, and have given preferential treatment to "regulars" in selection for specialized training courses.

In the years immediately following the end of Korean hostilities, reenlistment rates for regulars completing initial tours of duty proved to be disappointingly low, averaging less than 15 percent in 1954–55. This was due, in part, to the fact that many young men not normally on the "recruitment market," had enlisted in the Air Force or Navy during the Korean period in preference to being drafted in the ground combat arms. The high rates of personnel turnover resulting from these losses prompted the initiation of a wide range of programs designed to increase retention of qualified personnel. These included increased reenlistment bonuses in 1954; two major military pay laws, in 1955 and 1958; improvements in "fringe benefits" and military housing facilities; and a variety of administrative measures designed to enhance the career attractiveness of military service. These measures, as well as the gradual change in the composition of the enlistee groups, resulted in a significant increase in the "first-termer" reenlistment rate, to an average of 30 percent in 1959. This improvement has also been reflected in a steady increase in the size of the career enlisted force from about 530,000 in June, 1950, to 750,000 in December, 1954, and to about 1.0 million in December, 1958.[2]

Despite such improvement, the Armed Services have continued to be faced with the probability that the majority of their new trainees will leave military service after completing initial tours of duty. The difficulty has been intensified, moreover, by a persistent inverse relationship between technicality of skill and reenlistment rates. Since 1955, when occupational reenlistment rates were first reported, first-term reenlistment

[2] The "career" force is defined as consisting of personnel on second, or subsequent, terms of active duty. It is estimated on the basis of the number of personnel who have completed four or more years of military service.

rates have been consistently lowest among men in electronics and certain other highly technical skills, and highest in non-technical occupational groups such as food service and military police. This differential pattern has been related, in large part, to the fact that the Services have tended to select their best-educated recruits for training in the more technical skills; and that these personnel for various economic and socio-logical reasons have been least responsive to enlisted careers.

The training problem faced by the Armed Services, stemming from high rates of personnel turnover, can perhaps best be summarized by this comparison: The average working life expectancy of the eighteen-year-old civilian male worker has been estimated at 44.8 years by the Bureau of Labor Statistics, based on 1955 data. In contrast, on the basis of recent re-enlistment and attrition experience, we have estimated that the average active military service expectancy of the new enlistee, at the time of his entry into Service, is less than five years. The potential "return" on training investment is thus nearly ten times greater in the civilian economy than in the military.

A third and equally important set of considerations influencing military training programs relates to the mental aptitudes and educational level of the trainees. In civilian life, hiring standards are governed by job requirements and by practical labor market considerations. In the case of the Armed Services, however, public policy has dictated that broad considerations of equity also be recognized in establishing standards of selection for military service. Thus, in order to assure that the obligation of military service be shared as widely as possible, the Congress in 1951 set the minimum mental standard for induction at roughly the equivalent of a fourth-grade level of educational attainment. It was recognized at the time as undesirably low since it required acceptance of many individuals in the lowest acceptable mental category (Group IV) with little or no capability for specialized training.

The problem of low mental standards of acceptability was intensified by the cutbacks of total military strength following the end of Korean hostilities, and by the relatively high replacement needs of the Services for personnel with aptitudes for specialized training. Faced with a growing "qualitative gap" between job requirements and quality of personnel, the Department of Defense, beginning in 1955, authorized higher standards of acceptability for regular enlistees and encouraged large-scale programs for screening out personnel with limited training potential. In addition, under an amendment to the draft law enacted in 1958, mental standards for inductees were also raised by a requirement that registrants in Mental Group IV attain passing scores in a supplementary aptitude test battery before being accepted for induction.

A trend towards increased selectivity is evident in the altered distribution of new enlisted personnel by Mental Group since 1954. There was a sharp reduction in the acceptance of men in Mental Group IV, from 29 percent to 12 percent, and an increased concentration in Mental Group

III (or "average" category) from nearly 37 percent to 47 percent.

A similar improvement is indicated by trends in the over-all educational level of the enlisted force. In the Army, the percentage of enlisted men who were high-school graduates rose from 48 percent in December, 1952, to 61 percent in December, 1958. In the Air Force, the increase over the same period was from 64 percent to 75 percent. Comparable data are not at present available for the Navy or Marine Corps, but the trend has undoubtedly been in the same direction.

Although much of this increase in educational level was due to higher mental standards of selection and retention, the wide range of voluntary off-duty education programs for servicemen, supported by the Department of Defense, con-tributed to these gains. These include an extensive cor-respondence course program offered through the U.S. Armed Forces Institute, a Resident Center Program providing for college-level classroom courses at military posts or in nearby institutions, and Group Study Programs designed to fill a need for classroom education at sea or in areas where regular college facilities are not available. A total of about 240,000 servicemen were enrolled in these three programs in 1959.

Despite the very substantial improvement, it would be un-realistic to infer that the quality and educational level of personnel recently entering Service has reached an optimum level. The percentage of recruits who have enlisted before completing high school is still undesirably large. Moreover, the fact that the Services draw personnel from all sections of the nation, with widely divergent educational systems and standards, compels them to gear their training programs to a relative low "common denominator," which is probably much too elementary for some, while difficult for others.

Military Skill Training Programs

Faced with steady expansion of technical military skills and with high rates of personnel turnover, the Armed Services have in recent years been compelled to devote a sizable portion of their resources to in-service training programs. The task of transforming new recruits into seasoned fighting men and technicians has, in fact, become one of the primary peacetime missions of the military establishment.

Until recent decades, the limited needs of the Armed Services for trained specialists, which were not filled by direct recruitment of skilled workers from civilian life, were mainly met through informal on-the-job or apprentice-type training in military units. These gradual apprenticeship methods proved wholly inadequate, by themselves, to meet the urgent and more exacting skill requirements of our modern mechanized forces, particularly under mobilization conditions. Experience in World War I and World War II demonstrated the need for large-scale formal training programs to provide more intensive skill training to new recruits. An extensive network of Service schools was established which, in combination with supplementary civilian facilities, was equipped to train personnel in the full range of military specialties. These Service schools now constitute the primary vehicle for initial skill training in the Armed Services, particularly in the more technical skills.

Some indication of the size of the formal school training program of the Armed Services in recent years is provided by a special Department of Defense study made in 1956.[3] During the three-year period of Korean hostilities, a total of nearly 1.3 million servicemen, or more than 400,000 per year, received training in civilian-type specialties. This total, moreover, excludes combat training in purely military-type skills, flying training, professional training of officers, correspondence courses, and numerous short courses conducted at Navy bases or in informal troop schools. In 1955, the last year for which comparable data are available, the total number of trainees was 430,000. Since 1955 there has been some reduction in the absolute number of trainees due to reduced personnel intake, but the percentage of new personnel receiving initial school training has tended to increase, as a result of the need to assign an increasing proportion of new personnel to the expanding technical skill fields.

Despite the magnitude of these formal school programs, on-the-job training has continued to play an essential role in the overall process of military skill development. As in the civilian economy, many skilled military crafts can only be effectively acquired on-the-job, under actual operating conditions. This is true, for example, of the Navy deck ratings, such as Boatswain's Mates and Quartermaster's Mates, where shipboard apprenticeship is still considered the only method of acquiring the needed experience and "know-how."

For the more technical maintenance skills, many practical

[3] From report by the President's Commission on Veterans' Pensions, *Veterans in Our Society,* June 1956, House Com. Print No. 261, 84th Cong., 2d Sess., p. 47.

considerations also militate against attempting to develop a full-fledged journeyman or technician in the formal school system: the great diversity in types of equipment and in actual operating situations; the need to rotate and reassign personnel at periodical intervals; and in particular the short period of effective service available from most recruits. As a result, most entry-level training courses have as their objective the development of personnel qualified at an apprentice or junior level of skill, and rely on job training to develop the more specific skills needed to fully qualify at the journeyman level. In addition, advanced training is offered in Service schools, in civilian institutions, and through correspondence courses, designed to provide specialized training in new equipment or procedures and a broader technical foundation in various skills. These advanced courses have increased in relative importance in recent years, with the gradual growth in the number of career personnel, but still account for a modest share of the overall school training program.

As shown in Table IV, the proportion of enlisted personnel initially trained in Service schools, rather than in units, and the average length of the training courses, tend to vary directly with the technicality of the skill. In highly technical specialties, such as electronics maintenance, virtually all personnel are sent initially to school for courses averaging about one-half year in length. In contrast, less than half of the personnel assigned to clerical, crafts, or Services occupations received initial school training, in courses averaging between two and four months in length.

These occupational differences in training methods are

TABLE IV. *Percentage of Enlisted Personnel Initially Trained in Service Schools and Average Length of Training Courses by Major Occupational Group, 1956*

Occupational Group	Percent Trained	Average Length of Course (weeks)
Electronics	86	21
Electronics maintenance	98	28
Electronics Equipment operation	78	25
Other technical	73	15
Mechanics and repairmen	74	15
Administrative and clerical	47	10
Crafts	42	15
Services	40	9

broadly paralleled in the civilian economy. In general, formal training courses are also a major source of initial training of civilians, in the case of the newer technician skills, which require more theoretical background and an understanding of complex equipment. Formal training has continued to be relatively unimportant, however, in the more traditional skilled crafts, where apprenticeship or informal on-the-job training methods predominate.

In other respects, however, the content and methods of military training programs have differed substantially from their civilian counterparts. The short period of effective military service available from most recruits has imposed practical upper limits on the length of entry-level skill training. The tendency has, therefore, been to curtail or eliminate theoretical course content and to concentrate on the more immediate and practical elements of a relatively narrow job specialty.

As a result, the scope of most military courses in mechanical or technician skills is necessarily much more restricted than courses offered in technical institutes or similar civilian schools. For example, a typical civilian institute course in aircraft maintenance lasts for two full years. The graduate of such a course is considered qualified to perform all levels of maintenance on a variety of aircraft types with little or no technical supervision. A typical Air Force counterpart, the Apprentice Aircraft Mechanic Course on reciprocating engine aircraft, lasts only eighteen weeks. However, this course qualifies a graduate only to perform the more routine types of maintenance work under the direct supervision of a skilled mechanic, generally on a specific type of aircraft. An additional period of on-the-job experience of one year or more may be required before the apprentice Air Force mechanic can qualify as a "journeyman" in his more restricted specialty. Beyond that, broader training in advanced technical courses will be available to him if he chooses to reenlist and make the Air Force a career.

Similar contrasts may readily be drawn between Service school training in skilled crafts and civilian apprenticeship programs. For example, the Air Force offers a basic electrician's course of fourteen weeks duration, designed to train airmen in fundamentals of electricity and in techniques of electrical installation and maintenance. This training may be comparable to a high-school level vocational course but scarcely to a four-year civilian apprenticeship.

The very necessity to develop competent mechanics and

other skilled workers in short time periods has caused the military services to pioneer in a wide range of advanced skill training techniques. These have included use of training films, simulators, and many other types of training aids, and more recently extensive use of classroom television. One measure of the contribution of the Armed Services towards advancement of skill training methods is provided by the fact that, in 1957, over 1,000 training publications used in the Department of Defense were made available for inclusion in Training Materials Centers established by the Department of Labor, as part of that Department's program to strengthen the skills of the nation's work force.

Vocational Implications of Military Skill Training

From the foregoing summary, it is apparent that military skill training programs are geared, necessarily, to meet a special pattern of military job requirements. From the standpoint of the Military Services, the "return" on their training investment must be gauged by the extent to which this training contributes to the overall combat readiness of the Armed Services. One measure of this "return" is the fact that the Active military forces, at the end of the decade, included more than one million fully trained career enlisted men and officers, or about twice the number at the beginning of the decade. Another measure is the increase in the strength of the Reserve Forces, not on active duty, from a total of 2.6 million in June, 1950, consisting mainly of World War II veterans, to 4.4 million in June, 1959, including a much larger proportion of recent separatees from Service.

At the same time, the Armed Services have clearly made a substantial contribution to the vocational equipment of American youth and to the sum total of skills of the nation's civilian work force. Between July, 1950, and July, 1959, a total of over 6 million servicemen returned to civilian life after completing periods of military training and service. And, as we have seen, the great majority of these personnel received training in skills which have their counterpart in the civilian economy.

We have, unfortunately, only limited evidence as to the extent to which this military skill training has been directly used in later civilian employment. From earlier experience, we know that pilots trained in the Armed Forces during or after World War I served as the prime source of airline pilots in the expanding aviation industry. Similarly, a Bureau of Labor Statistics study conducted in 1952 revealed that 34 percent of all electronics technicians employed in the civilian economy, had been trained—in whole or in part—in Armed Forces technical schools, mainly during World War II.[4] (This, however, probably represented less than one-tenth of the total number of military personnel trained in electronics maintenance during the war.)

A more recent study, conducted for the Air Force in 1955, provides more specific information on the post-Service work experience of a sample of 5,000 airmen who had originally enlisted in 1950 and separated from the Air Force in 1954. The survey was confined to personnel in seven Air Force

[4] U.S. Bureau of Labor Statistics, *The Mobility of Electronic Technicians*, 1940–52, Bulletin No. 1150, p. 46.

career fields, ranging from highly technical skills, such as radio and radar maintenance, to nontechnical fields, such as supply and food service. On the basis of information obtained mainly from field interviews, the airmen were classified as to the relationship between their Air Force specialty and current occupation.

Some 17 percent in all seven fields had succeeded in getting a job considered to be related to their Air Force experience. The percentages varied widely among career fields, from 36 percent for radio and radar maintenance to only 4 percent in communications and 2 percent in air traffic control and warning. The low percentages in the latter skills are explained in large part by the limited availability of jobs such as air traffic control or radio operators in the civilian economy. The study also indicated a limited interest on the part of many youth in continuing in their military skills as a lifelong career. For example, two-thirds of those employed in food service jobs in the service did not attempt to get similar work in civilian life.[5]

The comparatively high percentage of former Air Force maintenance technicians who were reported working in related jobs in civilian life tended to confirm the observations of many military personnel officials that competition from civilian industry was a major factor in their high technician loss rates. These percentages, however, require some qualification. It is apparent from the survey report that a rather broad interpretation was placed on relationship between mili-

[5] Robert L. Thorndike and Elizabeth P. Hagen, *Attitudes, Educational Programs, and Job Experiences of Airmen Who Did Not Reenlist* (Air Force Personnel Training and Research Center, June, 1957).

tary and civilian jobs. For example, Air Force personnel trained in military electronic equipment maintenance (radio, radar, fire control equipment) were classified as working in the "same" or "closely related" jobs if they were subsequently engaged in a wide range of electrical repair jobs. In a much more restricted sense, the report notes that "a qualitative examination of the records does not indicate that many of these men are working in a civilian capacity on Air Force equipment supplied to the Air Force by civilian contractors. The men have scattered widely into a large number of companies and jobs, and are using their Air Force experience in many ways and in many settings." [6]

Despite the limitations in scope and timing of the statistics cited above, certain generalizations are indicated.

First, it is clear that a major contribution has been made by the Armed Services towards the training of men in electronics and in those other mechanical and technical skills which are most closely allied to the new military technology. It is probable, too, that many personnel trained in other older military skills which have civilian counterparts have also applied their training successfully in civilian life; however, statistical evidence on this score is lacking. In any event, they have accounted for a relatively smaller share of the trained labor force.

Secondly, there are broad contrasts between the military and civilian skill structures which militate against the ready transferability of skills. Many military skills, such as Army infantry or artillery crews, or Navy sonar operators, have no

[6] Thorndike and Hagen, *Attitudes, Programs, Experiences of Airmen*, p. 56.

civilian counterpart. Others, such as aircraft mechanics and electronics maintenance technicians, are required in much higher proportions in the Services than in the civilian economy. However, a rapidly expanding demand in some fields—such as electronics—may partly offset the disparity in total employment. In contrast, the Armed Services do not have occupational specialties directly comparable to those of farmers, sales workers, or manufacturing operatives.

Finally, the jobs to which men have been assigned in military service do not necessarily correspond to the occupations which they may wish to follow as life-long careers. This was particularly true during periods of large-scale mobilization and to a more limited degree during the Korean conflict, when many mature men, with established civilian work careers, were brought into military service. In more recent years, the increased reliance on voluntary recruitment, and the opportunities available to qualified enlistees to choose their occupational field and type of training, have made it possible for the Services to more closely match the individual's interests and special capabilities with his military job assignment. In fact, the opportunities available in military service to obtain this specialized training for possible later use in civilian life have been an increasingly important inducement for enlistment into military service.

As in the case of the young civilian worker, however, there is a "trial and error" process associated with occupational choice. The very process of training and working in a particular skill while in military service probably has influenced many young men to transfer into other lines of work after leaving military service. In fact, one of the more obvious reasons for failure to reenlist has been a desire to shift to a different occupation in civilian life.

On balance, we believe it reasonable to conclude that military skill training has made a direct and important contribution to the occupational skills of a significant minority of the youth who have returned to civilian life. It has been a major source of trained personnel in selected industries and occupations closely allied with military technology. In the case of many other youth, training in military skills has probably contributed more generally to their total knowledge and capabilities—including their hobbies and "do-it-yourself" activities—but has not found a direct and closely identifiable application in their civilian employment.

RELIGION AND YOUTH

by BENSON Y. LANDIS

CHILDREN AND YOUTH today live in a society in which there is considerable ferment regarding religion. The discussions are widespread both within and outside of religious circles. There are frequent references to large sums being expended for construction of new buildings for religious purposes, including the religious education of children and youth. The U.S. Department of Commerce estimates that these expenditures by religious bodies of all faiths were $863,-000,000 in 1958, $474,000,000 in 1953, $251,000,000 in 1948, and, omitting the war years when construction was restricted by regulation, $51,000,000 in 1938. Membership of some 250 religious bodies, reported by the official statisticians of all faiths, was, in round figures, 109,500,000 persons in 1958, 94,850,000 in 1953, 79,400,000 in 1948, 68,500,000 in 1940. Since 1940 the membership officially reported has increased much more rapidly than population. Books by religious leaders are found often on best-seller lists, and the sales of one

Benson Y. Landis is Director of the Bureau of Research and Survey of the National Council of Churches of Christ in the United States of America.

edition of the Bible since 1950 have made high records in the history of religious publishing.

However, there appears to be more enthusiasm over these figures from journalists than from professional churchmen or social scientists. The religious bodies do not record or report attendance at their services; they do not know what proportion of their members contribute money year by year; they do not generally state other evidence of the involvement of their members. While contributions to churches advance, so does the national income. Organized religion, so far as is now known, receives regularly one half of all sums given to philanthropy each year; and this amount is apparently steadily at about 1 percent of the disposable income of the people. If there has been a revival of religion, as some allege, there appears to be no increase in generosity of support of religion.

Among both religious leaders and social scientists one notes sharply diverse opinions concerning the recent developments in organized religion. One of the nation's noted theologians says that the United States is now both the most secular and the most religious nation. It is most secular, he writes, in the sense that people's important decisions frequently seem to be made without the guidance of the teachings of the historic religious; it is the most religious, he contends, because there is evidence of wide participation of lay people in the affairs of the religious organizations. An experienced clergyman says that official reports of church statistics convey impressions at variance with the experience of himself and of his colleagues while working among people.

In a prominent pulpit a clergyman who does much personal counseling preaches a sermon on religious revival and moral decline.

Members of religious bodies are largely "religious illiterates," says a religious educator at a seminar of specialists, and no one dissents. A well-known sociologist, studying democratic institutions, publishes an article entitled, "What Religious Revival?," and states that his weighing of evidence leads him to the conclusion that in the United States no fundamental long-time changes in religious interest or activity have occurred.

The dual role of religion in society is often described by the students of society. Religion makes for establishment of close ties between human beings—it is also a force making for division. Religion makes for the integration of the human personality, it is often testified; religious differences have also been cited as responsible for some of the bitterest antagonisms. There are undoubtedly universal elements in the teachings of the great religions; there are also emphases on uniqueness or distinctiveness that result in the separation of religious group from religious group. In our own communities we may see or hear about efforts for cooperation under religious auspices; we may also note the opposite. And religious differences, in our complex society, are observed to be "compounded" with other differences, such as those over power, economic position, social policies, or aims of education. Joseph Fichter, in *Sociology*,[1] says that in the United States

[1] Joseph H. Fichter, *Sociology* (Chicago: University of Chicago Press, 1957).

religious affiliation "conserves social status for the individual."

The foregoing is only a short reference to the current debate concerning religion in the United States. It is meant as a setting for the consideration of information on religion and youth that follows. This chapter will briefly interpret a variety of studies in the following fields, which obviously overlap to some extent: 1) The general experience of childhood and youth with respect to religion; 2) Participation of youth in the institutions of religion, particularly in the organizations for religious education, such as Sunday or Sabbath schools, day schools in which religion is taught, etc.; 3) Expressions by youth concerning standards commonly called religious, and opinions relating to religion; 4) Social conditions that affect the participation or functioning of youth in religious organizations.

Childhood and Adolescent Experiences

Young children form their ideas regarding religion with frail capacity and slight experience, and they gradually approximate the concepts of their elders, Allport writes in *The Individual and His Religion*.[2] Childhood experience, he says, is marked by fantasies and egocentrism. Inquiries are frequently put by small children to others. The children not only ask many questions in the realm of religion, even of theology, but they also expect prompt and precise answers. The child takes the religious practices that he sees about him for granted. Learning about religion is a "very subtle process,"

[2] Gordon W. Allport, *The Individual and His Religion* (New York: Macmillan, 1950).

however. Many children are disappointed with their early experience. Some drop references to religion at an early age, in part because they seem to find it of no immediate or practical aid.

More critical experiences with religion come during adolescence. Now the young person has more firsthand experience with the institutions of religion, assumes a more independent attitude, and often rebels against it. There is testimony that about two-thirds of adolescents assume some definite negative attitudes toward parental teachings of all kinds, including religion. Thus youth often change their earlier attitudes toward religion. Although the general tendency is for youth to enter the religious body of parents, there is some shifting of religious affiliation away from that of parents. Often, whether the young person shifts formal religion or not, doubts appear and are taken seriously, and he may drift into indifferent or opportunistic attitudes regarding the problems and issues of life. Opinions are frequently expressed to the effect that "modern youth" particularly have assumed these attitudes.

The days of adolescence are "days of decision," many researchers generalize. It is also called the "age of religious awakening" by Argyle in *Religious Behavior*.[3] This awakening, when it occurs, may be gradual or sudden. The sudden awakening or reconstruction of experience is often labeled "conversion." The frequency of conversion in our day, compared with earlier eras, cannot be definitely stated; frequency undoubtedly varies by regions and by cultural experience,

[3] Michael Argyle, *Religious Behavior* (Glencoe, Ill.: Free Press, 1959).

and by the practices of religious bodies. Apparently conversions frequently take place at about age sixteen, possibly at fifteen for girls.

When young people try to tell about their own religious experience during adolescence the writing becomes very varied, Professor Allport says. In this connection one must note that religious opinions are strongly influenced by other opinions, for example, artistic sentiments. Studies consulted seem to indicate that, of youth who profess to adhere to religious values, about 70 percent state that their awakening in adolescence was gradual, while the others went through marked crises or reported unusual emotional stimulation. But not all the decisions are in favor of religion; an unknown proportion of youth also make definite decisions away from adherence to the faith of their fathers or from that of their early childhood.

Participation

The extensive statistics officially reported reveal relatively wide participation by youth compared with ten or fifteen years ago. Children—including infants—and youth are on many rolls of church members, but there is no precise reporting of age groups by the religious bodies. Some crude estimates indicate that at least 20 percent of the 109,500,000 members of religious bodies may be under thirteen years of age. In the bodies that do not include children as members the practice is to admit persons at about age thirteen. Hence children and youth are often listed in the churches as full members. These national reports, however, say nothing about the quality or extent of involvement. It is probable that many youth contacts with institutions of religion—like those of adults—are altogether superficial.

The Protestant Sunday Schools report over 90 percent of all Sunday or Sabbath School enrollment in the country. Over 200 Protestant bodies reported 37,861,531 pupils in 1958, compared with 24,609,808 in 1945 (there was no enumeration in 1948). An analysis by age groups in 1957 revealed that only about 65 percent of the pupils were less than twenty-four years of age. The Protestant churches also reported 4,794 elementary and secondary *day schools* with a total enrollment of 358,739 pupils in 1958. About 80 percent of the enrollment—281,897—was in elementary schools, compared with 187,000 pupils in 3,000 elementary schools in 1952. There was no earlier enumeration of Protestant secondary schools. These reports appear in the annual *Yearbook of American Churches.*

According to the *Official Catholic Directory* there were 3,933,167 elementary school pupils in the Roman Catholic parochial day schools in 1958, and 783,155 pupils in secondary Catholic day schools, a total of 4,716,322 persons. By contrast, in 1948 there were 2,289,420 elementary day school pupils, and 506,397 in secondary schools, a total of 2,795,817. The Roman Catholic enrollment in the day schools in 1958 was equal to about 12 percent of total elementary and secondary school enrollment (public and private). Roman Catholic parishes are also required to give religious instruction to children in the public (tax-supported) schools. According to the *Directory* quoted there was 2,725,582 pupils in 1958, and 2,452,595 in 1948.

The "first national study of Jewish education in the United States," concentrating on elementary education, revealed 553,600 pupils aged five through seventeen in the Jewish schools of all types, and it was estimated that about 80 percent of all Jewish children receive "some Jewish schooling at some time during school age." In weekday afternoon schools were reported 47.1 percent of the total enrollment; in one-day schools in session either Saturdays or Sundays, 45.1 percent; and in day schools, 7.8 percent. Of all persons enrolled, 88.5 percent were in congregational schools, compared with 82.7 percent in 1948. A majority of pupils attend Jewish schools for three or four years. A majority of Jewish high-school youth do not receive religious education, it was stated in the report, *Jewish Education in The United States.*[4] According to the *American Jewish Yearbook* (1950) there were 258,052 pupils in schools in session either Saturdays or Sundays; rapid development during and after World War II was reported in that book.

The literature of specialists studying Protestant and Jewish education particularly reveals wide variance in stated goals, even within the same denomination, and varying emphases on method. Probably there would be wide agreement with a generalization by an educator that much religious education is "like a shallow river, 'a mile wide and an inch deep.'"

[4] Alexander M. Dushkin and Uriah Z. Engelman, *Jewish Education* (New York: American Association for Jewish Education, 1959).

In a national sample of 1,925 adolescent girls in grades six to twelve, in a study made for the Girl Scouts, 52 percent reported that they belonged to "some church group." [5] Of girls over sixteen, 55 percent belonged to a church group, of those aged eleven and under, only 24 percent belonged to some church group or club.

Standards and Opinions

When youth are queried about religion they generally state their adherence to the traditional religious teachings in our society, but at the same time many who profess adherence are not actively expressing their religious convictions and a considerable proportion of these reveal themselves confused concerning the place of religion both in their own lives and in the communities in which they live. In this section "summaries of summaries" of various studies will be given.

Of a sample of 10,000 teen-agers in metropolitan Chicago it is reported that the majority professed adherence to the historic faiths. Those queried were a broad sample of the teen-agers of the metropolitan area, and thus included persons from every major religious group and persons with no affiliation. About one-third, however, felt confused in their religious beliefs. One-third agreed with the following statement: "Men working and thinking together can build a good society without any divine or supernatural help"; one-third were undecided; one-third disagreed. Seventy-three percent did not agree with this statement: "The more I learn about

[5] Survey Research Center, Institute for Social and Religious Research, *Adolescent Girls* (Ann Arbor, Mich.: University of Michigan, 1956).

science, the more I doubt my religious beliefs." Seventy-one percent said they would like to have more information about religion than they had. About 41 percent said they were still searching for beliefs that would "make sense to them." [6]

In "Elmtown," a Midwestern corn belt community, 735 adolescent boys and girls were reported by A. B. Hollingshead as usually accepting the religion of their parents.[7] Formal religious training begins in the Sunday school. However, only one-half of the high-school students actually participated in religious activities. To 90 percent of the boys and to 80 percent of the girls religion did not have a "compulsive quality." To these youth religion did not appear to have specific content or meaning. Adolescents were interested in their church groups or classes more for social than for religious purposes. Ministers were concerned about the "loss" of young people from church life. There were also open conflicts between the recreational practices of young people and the standards of some clergymen. Adolescents hid many of their activities from their parents, teachers, and clergymen.

When 2 percent of the homes in Kalamazoo, Mich. were visited by volunteer interviewers, it was found that over half the parents were members of various religious bodies, and about one-third of the total number of families reported that they had special problems with religious activities for their children and themselves during the summer. Low-income people reported the most problems. Church-goers had prob-

[6] Y.M.C.A. of Metropolitan Chicago, *The Youth of Chicagoland: A Study of Its Attitudes, Beliefs, Ideas, and Problems* (1958). Mimeographed.
[7] A. B. Hollingshead, *Elmtown's Youth* (New York: Wiley, 1949).

lems just as often as nonchurch goers, and the number who felt a need for guidance was not significantly lower among church affiliated families. The interviewers suggested that summer is becoming "increasingly a period of total family activity." People of all faiths and none were questioned.[8]

More than 1,000 boys and girls in junior and senior high schools in Oklahoma, when asked to state their "areas of concern and problems," rated "religious problems" below several others. Fifty-five percent of senior high-school youth interviewed attended church and 55 percent attended Sunday School. Those making the study reported that little interest was shown by youth in understanding democracy.[9]

The ability of 915 Roman Catholic girls in eleventh grade to apply the principles of the moral law to actual and hypothetical life situations was studied by Carmen V. Diaz.[10] Five hundred of the girls were in diocesan high schools and the remainder were in the public schools of New York and New Jersey. All the girls received religious training. Those in diocesan high schools received the regular instruction given there and those in public schools attended the instruction given in parishes for Catholics in public schools. Various tests were given. In general, it was concluded that

[8] Lauris Whitman, Helen F. Spaulding, and Alice Dimock, A Study of the Summertime Activities of Children in Relation to the Summer Program of the Churches (New York: National Council of Churches, 1959). Mimeographed.

[9] Lloyd Estes et al., Teen-Age Frontiers Survey, 1953. Unpublished. Summarized in Richard E. Hamlin, Hi-Y Today (New York: Association Press, 1955).

[10] Carmen V. Diaz, A Study of the Ability of 11th Grade Girls to Apply the Principles of the Moral Law to Actual and Hypothetical Life Situations (New York: Fordham University, 1952). Dissertation.

Catholic girls in eleventh grade possessed the ability to apply the principles of the moral law as taught by that church. However, no significant difference was found between the scores of those girls who had eleven years of religious training and those who had three to six years of training.

"Religion is at the center of the total function of the Roman Catholic parochial school," Joseph Fichter writes after a team of researchers studied St. Luke's elementary school in a Midwestern city. Many aspects of the life of the school and of the attitudes of the 632 pupils are interpreted, and some comparisons are made with 180 Catholic pupils in a public school. "The religious practices and groups of St. Luke's school are interwoven with the whole educational program. They are themselves educational since they are designed to assist in the promotion of the 'different kind' of education that parochial school children obtain. It would be unthinkable to the teaching staff of the school to separate religion from education, or to suggest either that religion interferes with the school or that the school interferes with religion." The public school pupils attended the weekly classes in religion provided by the parish for children not in the parochial school.

Catholic children in parochial and in public schools were found to have "quite similar" tastes and preferences. They nominated the "same great historical persons in the same order." There appeared to be "little difference between parochial and public school children" in standards of conduct as measured by a personality test that did not include reference to religious convictions or supernatural motivation, "the

area in which the parochial school pupils are at their best."
The Catholic children in both schools "accept and demonstrate, in about the same proportions, the virtues of honesty,
obedience, gratitude, self-control, and kindliness."

"The greatest difference between the two schools is the
fact that parochial school children explain their attitudes
most often with religious and supernatural reasons." Another
difference was that parochial school children expressed more
favorable opinions toward labor unions and the foreign aid
program of the United States. Parochial school children in
the community studied appeared to receive a broader social
education than the Catholic children in public school.

The parochial school is described as "the largest single
focus for cooperation" among the church members, and as
an "example of successful voluntary association." [11]

Polls of 11,000 children of elementary school grades receiving instruction in Jewish schools, recorded by Dushkin
and Engelman revealed the following results: 6 out of 10
of the children reported that they "liked their Jewish school
and would go if given free choice." Nine out of 10 children
"accept Jewish education as natural and desirable in the
American environment where, they say, all children should
receive some form of religious education." However, a poll
of 1,560 adult Jewish community leaders revealed that 75
percent were opposed to the full-time Jewish day school,
which enrolls only 7.8 percent of all Jewish pupils receiving
religious instruction.

[11] Joseph H. Fichter, *Parochial School* (Notre Dame, Ind.: University
of Notre Dame Press, 1958).

Protestant youth who are in senior high school and in older age brackets, and who are also in church youth organizations, rate their churches favorably but say that they have in their churches few opportunities to put into action the convictions and attitudes that they had acquired through religious activities. A broad sample of 1,667 youth in 188 local churches was studied by Helen F. Spaulding and Olga Haley.[12] Relatively few reported opportunities for meeting or working with youth of denominations other than their own. In general they thought that adults in the churches wanted youth to participate and valued the opinions of youth in the program of the local churches. The youth asked for adult leaders with more training than those they had. In many churches the youth program was reported to be "very limited."

The relation of youth's personal adjustment problems to ten teachings of the church of the Brethren, a Protestant denomination, were considered by A. Stauffer Curry.[13] He secured information from 505 Brethren youth and 388 in interchurch Protestant groups, all being fifteen to twenty-four years of age. The Church of the Brethren teaches its youth not to smoke, not to go to the movies, not to dance. The study indicated that 57 percent of the Brethren youth indicated that they had "problems" engendered by the church teaching against participation in dancing, 29 percent in con-

[12] Helen F. Spaulding and Olga Haley, A Study of Youth Work in Protestant Churches (New York: National Council of Churches, 1955). Mimeographed.
[13] A. Stauffer Curry, But To Understand: An Analysis of Youth's Personal Problems As They Relate to 10 Social Practices (Elgin, Ill.: Brethren Publishing House, 1953).

nection with attending movies, and 18 percent with smok-
ing. In most instances lower proportions of interchurch
groups reported such problems.

"While young people in the Y.M.C.A. accept (or rather
assent to) traditional religious beliefs, these beliefs exist on
the whole as part of a vague set of ideas which are not incorporated into the lives of the large majority of young
people. Few young people take these beliefs seriously enough
so as to use them as the main directive for their lives. The
major interest of youth seems to be focused on carving out a
little area of life in which there is security for themselves
and their families. Deep concern for the welfare of others
and desire to participate vigorously in community development is shown only by a small minority." With these words
Murray G. Ross sums up studies of 1,935 youth, constituents
of city Y.M.C.A.s throughout the country,[14] of whom 80
percent were male and 50 percent had been to college. All
were in the eighteen to twenty-nine year age group; 34 percent were Roman Catholics, 59.1 percent, Protestant, 3.5
percent, Jewish, and the remaining unclassified.

A marked increase in professed commitment to religious
values is reported after comparing tests of groups of college
students at Ohio State University over three decades, 1929
to 1958.[15] In 1958 there was much more severe moral judgment about the statement, "disbelieving in God," than in

[14] Murray G. Ross, *Religious Beliefs of Youth* (New York: Association Press, 1950).
[15] Solomon Rettig and Benjamin Pasamanick, "Changes in Moral
Values Over Three Decades," *Social Problems*, VI (Spring, 1959).

1929, but only slightly more than in 1939 and 1949. The same tendency is noted in severe moral judgment about the statement, "not giving to support religion when able." Moral values do undergo change, the investigators conclude. In 1959 they report that there appears to be an increase in severity of moral standards in those matters "that may be associated with the sanctity of the individual life, and those that assure the basic democratic form of voting behavior."

"The Jewish [college] student sincerely believes that his home has been the major factor in influencing his Jewish attitudes." He thinks that Jewish students who participate in Jewish organizations "have been influenced in their Jewish thinking by such participation." "He does feel that his formal Jewish education has had much effect on him." "His college experience has weakened his religious interest." The student "grows more and more eager for social and cultural contact with the larger world, and seeks to broaden the local, narrow concerns of family and religion." Thus does Leon Feldman sum up for general readers many studies of the personal attitudes and values of Jewish college students.[16]

Some disaffection of college youth from formal religious life seems to occur in all faiths, Gordon W. Allport concludes. However, after years of rebellion against traditional forms many young people return to these same forms. But some of those returning show only vestiges of loyalty or main-

[16] Leon Feldman, "The Jewish College Student," *Jewish Spectator* (December, 1955). A more technical paper is his "The Personality of the Jewish College Student" presented before Yivo Social Science Circle, New York, June 6, 1956.

tain only nominal connections with religious organizations. He also records his opinion that college students are in the main ignorant of the writings of the great theologians and of those "brilliant minds" that have engaged in strenuous thinking as they have wrestled with the critical issues of life and "the attainment of religious maturity."

Social Conditions Affecting Participation

The functioning of youth in religious organizations is reported to be related to such factors as class, mobility, and the rise of the suburb.

Of Elmtown's youth, A. B. Hollingshead wrote: "Nonparticipation [in religious organizations] is very strongly associated with lower class, and participation with higher class position. The students who participate in religious organizations carry the class system into the church; consequently religious clubs are class biased." In Elmtown, 51 percent of the high-school students had no active connection with the town's religious bodies.

"The kind of religion to which one belongs both reflects the social status of the individual and contributes to his status," Joseph Fichter writes in *Sociology*. "The conservative and traditional churches which pursue their functions unobtrusively and do not put great demands upon their members are typical of high-status religions. They represent a kind of haven for the energetic and harassed American. They provide reassurance and comfort and satisfy the important American quest for security. It is as though everything else must change but these upper-class religions must remain stable. . . . Religion is the slowest-changing major institution in the American culture. The religious groups, especially those which have the highest aura of social prestige and respectability, tend to conform to, rather than to change, the secular milieu in which they exist."

The high mobility of Americans and the resulting "rootlessness" are often remarked. This mobility is of two kinds: horizontal or geographical, and vertical. The first type, involving frequent movement from community to community is thought by many to weaken the traditional family system, but the precise deleterious effects on the family, or youth specifically, are difficult to ascertain. Mobility, it is also stated, makes for affiliation with religious bodies—when people reach a new community they wish to have a few friends and one way to acquire them is to attend religious services.

Vertical mobility, movement up or down in the social scale, is also a marked characteristic in our modern life. This social mobility tends to disturb "family solidarity," Sidney Aronson writes.[17] Desire for success, according to American standards, is often cited as a force for changing social status. Change of social status makes for "social distance" between members of families. Mr. Aronson mentions a mother who said she felt comfortable only "in the home of the son who had not gone to college." Professor Fichter also considers the common desire for "upward social mobility." Our economy has offered varied opportunities to our people. Not only

[17] Sidney Aronson, *Religious Revival and Jewish Family Life* (New York: Synagogue Council of America, 1957). Mimeographed.

the immigrant but also the native American, he says, strives to "go as high as his competence will allow." He states that the opportunity for lay participation in religious institutions "also provides an avenue for upward social mobility." "A person may gain social recognition through these activities when he finds himself blocked and frustrated in the secular channels of mobility. Many of the functions thus performed are in essence secular but they are given an extra value in that they are being done 'for the church.'"

In the rapidly expanding suburbs many local religious organizations are growing rapidly and many new structures are being built; moreover, here is the focus of the interest of experienced churchmen who are concerned about the quality of local religious life. Speaking before the Synagogue Council of America, Rabbi Albert I. Gordon made generalizations about the suburbs which probably receive wide agreement from Jewish and other religious leaders.[18] Many activities are being carried on with the synagogue as the center. Great strides forward are being made in religious education. There are "superior" buildings for the teaching of religion to children. Women appear to have assumed new positions of leadership in families. But he says that evidence of commitment to the historic religion is such that "we are forced to admit the synagogue is far from witnessing a revival of religion." Writers belonging to other denominations mention many activities in suburban churches, strong local institu-

[18] Albert I. Gordon, *What Do We Know About American Jewish Life As It Affects the Jewish Religious Scene?* (New York: Synagogue Council of America, 1957). Mimeographed. See also this author's *Jews in Suburbia* (Boston: Beacon Press, 1959).

tions, much emphasis on buildings and organization, but little evidence of dedication to the historic standards of the religions.

There are "two worlds of church life in the United States," Glen W. Trimble writes; the metropolitan and the non-metropolitan.[19] A study of 114 religious bodies for 1953 reveals that 46 percent of the Protestants, 75 percent of the Roman Catholics, and 98 percent of the Jews, live in the standard metropolitan areas. In the metropolitan areas are 29 percent of the local Protestant churches and 50 percent of the local Roman Catholic churches. Protestant membership is highest, in relation to total population, in the South, and lowest in the Northeast, while the Roman Catholic situation is the reverse.

Summary

There is wide public discussion of religion, with sharply varying opinions among both laymen and social scientists with respect to the religious interest of people. The author agrees with the statement that probably no fundamental long-time changes have occurred. Religion is both a uniting and a divisive force in society.

Young children usually take for granted the religious practices they see around them and assume the beliefs of their elders. Adolescence is a time of awakening, of decision, and of significant rebellion against traditional religion. For many decades college experience has been resulting in weakening

[19] Glen W. Trimble, "Two Worlds of Church Life in the United States," Information Service, National Council of Churches, XXXVIII, No. 7. (March 28, 1959).

commitment to historic faiths in an undetermined proportion of students, but many of these later return to participation in religious organizations.

The numbers of pupils receiving religious education in the
institutions of the three major faiths were much higher in
1958 than in 1948. Much of the education that goes on is
superficial, however, and many contacts of children and youth
with these schools are also superficial, according to the testimony presented here.

Most youth, when questioned or tested express accord with
traditional beliefs or principles, but fewer of them participate
in religious organizations and actively implement their ideals,
according to reports here reviewed. One study of college
students at a state university comparing present values with
those of prior decades indicates that there is now more
acceptance of religious values.

The functioning of youth in religious organizations is frequently along class lines. Much concern is stated by religious
leaders about mobility, and "rootless" people. The growing
suburbs are marked by many activities for all age groups in
religious organizations, but experienced observers do not
report a "revival" of commitment to historic religion there.

THE CHILD AS POTENTIAL

by GARDNER MURPHY
and LOIS BARCLAY MURPHY

THE CONCEPT of the child as potential is challenging—so challenging, indeed, that it is threatening, so limited are our resources to deal with the problem, potential for *what?* As a culture oriented toward universal education and the promotion of knowledge regarding health and growth, we have made progress in promoting the child's potential as a physical and intellectual being. In what terms are we to think ahead about the child's potential in a technological, atomic, space-expanding, and, from a military point of view, potentially explosive era?

Knowledge of nutrition, vitamins, and minerals, together with the achievements of miracle drugs, have saved lives of children, contributed to increased growth and physical strength in the last few generations. A parallel task for the next generations is that of making available resources to salvage and help to social usefulness thousands of children unnecessarily doomed by preventable retardation and emo-

Gardner Murphy is Director of Research and Lois Barclay Murphy is Research Psychologist at the Menninger Foundation, Topeka, Kansas.

tional disturbance. Many of these are highly sensitive children with potentials for a good life and important contributions. Today we have the paradox that expert knowledge has produced extraordinary results in salvaging the potentialities of *some* crippled, cerebral palsied, polio, and brain damaged children. But these technical resources are not yet available for all.

We are just beginning to learn that some psychogenically retarded, autistic and intellectually blocked children, can be helped to become the actively functioning sensitive people they are capable of being. We are learning that sensory deprivation in infancy, lack of adequate mothering, traumatic separation, or institutionalization can cripple the physical, mental, or emotional development of babies; but we have not yet achieved the professional resources or the institutional changes required to prevent such unnecessary losses. We need more research, concerning both prevention and therapy, on all groups of children whose development has been disturbed by inadequate nurturing, traumatic interruptions, or illnesses; we have much to learn about sensitivity and vulnerability and ways of strengthening and promoting growth in sensitive children. We are concerned, however, not only with the unusual child but with the everyday child whose individual pattern of weaknesses, strengths, talents, limitations, individual drives, and social belongingness requires equally skilled guidance and understanding.

Second, we may be concerned with his potential as a member of a community that may be very different from the one in which he is growing up. This includes his potential contribution to the solutions of the staggering problems which confront this rising generation, his potential as a clear, honest, courageous analyst of the issues which will confront him in domestic and international relations, and himself as a potential component and creative shaper of a democratic society gradually outgrowing injustices and self-contradictions and achieving a group life which is fulfilling to its members and capable of carrying itself forward through years of dynamic change.

Third, we are interested in his fulfillment as contributor to the destiny of American life—contributor in biological terms as parent, ultimately ancestor, with the personality riches of wide and freely emancipated potentialities which belong to each person, and free contributor toward the cultural trends which have long-range viability and promise in a maturing democratic society.

Who knows enough to tell how to realize such potentialities? The only realistic thing we can do is to suggest directions in which present research points, issues that cannot lightly be dismissed, areas in which one might look for more information, problems with which parents, educators, and community members must wrestle.

The Child Should Choose

Our first tentative reply is this: Since no one can tell us in full, let us begin by noting and studying what the child can tell us. Perhaps in many ways—through all his inarticulateness, his nonverbal communication, his gestures, tears, clenched fist, sleeplessness, or, on the other hand, radiant joy and deep relaxed absorption into himself—he can point the direction in which we might give him more of what he seems to need in order to grow in a balanced, resilient, creative way. The first answer then well might be: Let us give positive response to that which the child himself positively emphasizes. No answer is final: The child may in his anguish seem first of all to need self-justification or even revenge, a need which would be slight or nonexistent if somehow his life could be better structured. Our thesis is simply that it is better to let the child tell us what he positively craves; indeed, if we do not respond to his joys and resentments, if we do not take his feelings seriously, we have no full or clear picture. We must be alert to notice signs of his cravings for companionship, for social understanding, for skills, for an understanding of the physical world, the living world, the esthetic and scientific world, the social and personal world. If his mind is not free to reach out and immerse itself in the things which mean most to him, we are unlikely to be able to guide him well.

First of all, then, in answer to the question which of the child's potentials shall we accent at any given time, "Let the child choose." Let us learn from his choices where his interests and talents lie in terms of what he is ready for, can use for growth at a given time, what his pace, potential depth, and range are. He may need support and help in sustaining an interest, in developing the techniques he needs in order to carry it through. But if it is *his* interest, goal, longing, there will be an optimal chance for fullest growth of his potential capacity.

Many everyday questions may be involved here. Does the child need freedom or discipline? Since patently most children need some of both and, indeed, ask for both, and since the answer regarding the proportions and areas of each depends upon age level, temperament, previous development, and the subtleties of present-day personality interactions in family and community, we would say: Let the child, through his behavior, through his emotional responses, through his rigidities, apathies, gaiety, impulsive animal spirits, tension or relaxation, his tendency to function best in a given balance of external control and autonomy, tell us what doses of freedom and of discipline he may be able to use and where, and when.

Some children need more free time, free from adult coercion; some children need more supervision, guidance, and control. In both instances we would try to avoid the dangers of a casualness which seems to mean lack of interest and, on the other hand, the type of supervision which the child experiences as nagging and coercive. Again, there may be overstimulation and continuous pressure through excessive demands, or understimulation in which the child's struggle to take in the meaning of the world or to master it, his eagerness for contact with richer experience, is ignored to the point of "deprivation." The amount of freedom a child can use depends in part on his ability to grasp and to organize situations for himself; the amount of structure or formal organization he needs depends in part on the level of complexity, confusion, or tension which would exist without adult directives and the child's capacity to handle the complexity of confusion constructively. The work of Kurt Lewin and his associates showed that for many children both laissez-faire and autocratic methods produced tense, frustrated, hostile feelings, while democratic guidance produced the most co-operative attitudes and the best achievements. The degree of satisfaction, integration, and progress in achieving goals shown by the child will indicate whether the balance he has is good for him.

Differences in Potential

Again with reference to encouragement of and concentration upon the child's potential strengths rather than his weaknesses, experience with individual children's responses to adult ways of handling this problem can be profoundly helpful. When we speak of developing potentialities, we do not mean to advocate pushing individual talents to a degree that prevents healthy development of the whole personality. Many gifted people, like John Stuart Mill, Ruth Slenczynska, and Norbert Wiener, have regretted as adults the forced and excessively concentrated focus on specialized achievement which kept them from normal childhood, and either necessitated great adjustments as adults or impoverished their whole adult life. There has to be room for the growing period, with all its needs, for adequate opportunity for maturation and experience in each area of the personality, and for a chance to grow into the human family. The child may tell us that he needs music or science, or craftsmanship, as many a biography has made clear; but many a talented child also needs a range of social contacts and social acceptance, a range of normal experiences serving as context for the delight in a specialized gift.

Nor can we assume out of hand that every child has some one outstanding potential gift and proceed simply to emphasize that, or assume that all children have potentialities in every area. Some children show from early years a well-balanced capacity for growth at a healthy but moderate level, where other children show wide irregularities in development. With this second group there is always the question, how can the strengths of such children be developed without ignoring and therefore increasing their relative weaknesses? How can they be strengthened in the weak spots, without depriving the special abilities of a chance to mature?

These are not easy questions to answer. We cannot demand perfection, and may need to settle for compromises made with the best judgment available in reference to each particular child. The whole issue would be much less painful to children and ultimately to ourselves if we could modify our often bleak, rigid, mechanical concepts of normality (our concern with "the normal range") so that individuals would feel less self-conscious and embarrassed by relative weaknesses in one or more areas. Holding a child to high standards need not constrict his personality if the standards are within his reach—if his muscles, visual, and auditory equipment, maturity of differentiation, and capacity for integration are "ready" to meet the demands that are made. And the development of social strengths does not preclude full use of a child's talents, capacity for mastery, for creativity, for scientific achievement if the latter are not emphasized in an isolating way or conceived as special and differentiating the child from other children. We might, indeed, take a lesson from some other countries, such as India, where there seems to be more tolerance of individual variation, and where "norms" of development are certainly very much less coercive.

Such individual differences, together with the paucity of our knowledge, mean that some loss can be expected to accompany each gain. In some modern schools, where there is strong emphasis on intellectual curiosity, individuality in painting, storytelling, dramatic expression, and imagination in contriving and carrying out science experiments, the children do, indeed, appear to be more goal-minded and creative than children in group-oriented schools. But in some research studies these creative, goal-minded children appear to show considerable tension, and one could raise the question whether it is sound to put demands for originality on all of the children at seven or eight. At a period when children need to become aware of themselves, aware of the individualities of other children about them, aware of the nature of childish as contrasted with adult interests and modes of thought and feeling, some have a special need for fuller group participation. The development of potentials, then, means the study of the right time for different degrees of emphasis between individualized and socialized capacities in different children.

The question of providing for range as against narrow concentration is not simple. Hackneyed terms of this sort are misleading. There are children who need above all to discover their own potential in terms of depth, in terms perhaps of a single deep and overwhelming intellectual, esthetic, or social form of self-fulfillment, or the discovery of their powers. There can be danger in filling up such a child's life with a diversity of scheduled activities, with a succession of clubs, sports, and lessons to the point at which the child says, "The one thing that interests me now is just to paint and paint and paint." Or, as another child said, "There isn't any place for myself."

This does not mean that the child can always accurately assay the consequences of today's activity. His concentration on one activity may not be productive, but may be a substitute for other satisfactions he is afraid to pursue. He may drive himself beyond the safety point into hypertension and sleeplessness. He may fray the edge of his own margin to the point of exhaustion. This means only that we should try to receive *all* of the child's testimony and let it consolidate itself and become clear before we think of turning a deaf ear to it; that we always find eyes and ears for the testimony of the hidden potential as well as for the overt expression of the child who has learned so well what it is that we want to hear, what it is that meets the norms and requirements which in the long run are deemed appropriate for an age group or a community group. A flower or a tree cannot tell us articulately what it needs for growth, but can still tell us a great deal. We ask only that the child be watched as closely as a flower or a tree would be when new soils, new methods of handling are being considered. Indeed, the child would soon be telling us more articulately how we can help him to realize his potential and—what is often forgotten—how we can help organize or define the environment, the round of duties, the world of social give and take, so that it can be most fulfilling to him.

We can not only give him resoluteness in facing walls that are hard to scale; we may, when walls are being used only to butt his head against, find ways to help him get over or around the walls, or occasionally help him to blast through or rebuild the more fundamental architecture of his life. In the "inner-directed" world of David Riesman's pioneers, the aim was always to batter down the opposition. Today, along with such an emphasis, we realize that the demands of many a child's environment are sometimes too much for him, sometimes too little, and that hand-in-hand with the realization of inner potentials goes the rebuilding of the world in such a way that more children can more adequately realize what is inarticulate within them.

The Individual and the Group

This has been an "individual-centered" plea. Children's needs are complex and manifold. Children vary beyond all possibility of adequate description, and there is no likelihood that in our generation we shall know how to set free the potentials of each. The other chapters in this symposium will help us to grasp how scant our knowledge of genetics remains today and therefore how scant our understanding of the basic human biology of the growth potential; they will indicate how limited is our knowledge of the basic laws of social and cultural dynamics upon which individual fulfillment must depend. We must, however, do our best now as we shift to another primary emphasis of this brief discussion: Emphasis upon the reciprocity of individual and social world, shared feelings of belonging to family and group, the ways in which the individual can best be fulfilled by attending to a unit larger than the individual, namely, the parent-child or whole-family patterns and the family-family or community, national and international pattern upon which, in this interdependent world, each individual's fulfillment must necessarily depend.

It is not difficult to construct a bridge from our concern with individuality to our concern with group membership, for, as already hinted, many a child tells us that his greatest need, his greatest unfulfilled potential, lies in the area of "feelings of belonging." Just as he may want an opportunity to exercise free imagination with a chance for creative thought and experience, so he may want most of all the feeling of easy friendly interchange, the sense of knowing how to achieve normal acceptance. "Feelings of rejection" are very common not only among children brought to clinics for therapy but even in family circles in which it is taken for granted that "of course the child knows we love him"; and feelings of rejection in the elementary-school period and in adolescence are very widely reported in our culture, possibly intensified by conditions of individual competitiveness which have dominated the American cultural scene.

At any rate, to push the child into social interaction is a very different thing from studying his social hungers, the terms in which friendship and participation are possible for him, his troubles in achieving acceptance, his inability to accept the pushing which parents and teachers often regard as their duty. A social world dominated by technological progress runs the risk of losing the human insight and sensitivity needed to make social gains on this planet during the space age. The foundations for this sensitivity and insight have to be laid in the very beginnings of personality development through shared feeling and understanding—first between mother and small child, then through the whole family, and in school, and in the major settings of the child's life.

Margaret Fries' article on the relation between early personality development and the difficulty of international cooperation did not concern itself just with the occasional Hitler or McCarthy, but with the problem of hostility and aggression rooted in childhood, as it distorts or disturbs all levels of political action in adult life. Here we need to recognize individual differences in thresholds for frustration, in tendencies to respond to frustration by aggression, in tendencies to develop or to accumulate potentially explosive reservoirs of aggressive tensions, persistent overt or covert hostile attitudes, and differences in the ways in which the child's experiences channel these into constructive or destructive directions. Just as nuclear reactivity can be used to destroy civilization with hydrogen bombs or to provide new dimensions of constructive energy, so the energy generated in the interaction of personalities may destroy nations or lead to new levels of culture. We know that the will to attack can be directed against disease, slums, flood areas, or ignorance; it can save instead of destroying.

Some studies of children in contemporary families show that it is possible to keep warmth in family living, strong family loyalty, the father's sense of closeness to all the family, the mother's concern with each child's needs despite the pressures of modern technical and competitive patterns associated with high living standards, labor-saving devices, and community activities. There seems to be no doubt that the strong patterns of family life still evident in the United States, where family solidarity means at-homeness, an inner sense of "knowing who you are" and delight or pride in family membership, may often accomplish what cannot be accomplished by any amount of experience outside the family. It may be that the neighborhood and community experience can most effectively permit the extension of the first family experiences, the feeling of resonance to and capacity to identify with other human beings, and that the school years—if there is not too much moving from one neighborhood to another, with its often disturbing change of friendship patterns—gradually allow the first family warmth to suffuse other relationships.

There is a place for planned social experiences in the elementary-school years and in the high-school years. Such planning, however, is likely to be effective only in the context of the consolidation of the family experiences and community experiences which precede them, and only when care is taken not to demand the same vigorous pace, the same

quick socialization and social reciprocity of all children without reference to backgrounds. Too much planned activity in
an institutional setting may actually attenuate or jeopardize
the family life which was and is still needed to feed the roots
of warm relationships.

It has often been contended that commercial amusements
may break up family living. It is equally true that shared
commercial amusements may under certain conditions keep
family members together, not only physically but personally.
The important point is not what the leisure time activity is,
but what it means to the child eager to share his interests
and eager likewise to gain respect for those interests which
may at the time transcend or overflow the group standard.

The Child and the Community

There is no "one-way street" for what the community can
offer the child without reference to what the child can offer
the community. Research has led us to see that the desire
and the ability of the child to give is just as important as his
ability to receive; that his generosities are far from artificial
products of teaching or sheer desires to repay what has been
received, to liquidate a debt or reduce a sense of guilt. The
child may enjoy giving and sharing as intensely as he does
anything in life. Family participation in community life
can evoke this two-way sense and can make for joy in the
child if he can contribute something to the joy of others.
Informal opportunities to help other children or the more
formal efforts through the teaching of geography and the
social studies may help children to "feel with" the children

of other communities or countries. It is not only at the time of a "drive," or Christmas gift campaign, or disaster relief or other community crises that we can accentuate the sense of being one with the group, being a contributing participant in its life as well as receiving from it.

In India and other developing countries children can sometimes participate in basic community tasks of construction and reconstruction—opportunities denied to children in our rich, advanced, country. Modern education seems at times to have forgotten the important distinction between individual mental hygiene and capacity for social participation. While it is assumed that the mastery of stress or the reduction of anxiety is a therapeutic problem independent of community organization, it is also sometimes assumed that socialization, in the sense of free interchange of ideas and feelings in the group, is an automatic guarantee against loneliness and insecurity. The problems are too intricate for such a summary. Children differ too much, communities differ too much, for such a cliché to be useful. We can, however, say that the problem of helping the child to give to the family, to the neighborhood, to the community, to the nation, and to the world, helping the child to find deep satisfaction in what he can contribute, is just as basic a need in this era as the need to free the individual from misunderstandings, rigidities, and tensions. There is just as great an unfulfilled potential in the matter of warm, generous membership in a community as there is in neglected science and art talents. There is as big a need to study, understand, and develop the child's potential for happy social living as there is a need for the child to develop and utilize special skills. Some children need a definite structure and organization to help consolidate feelings of belonging; letting such a child struggle by himself can reinforce his isolation. For others the structural requirements are slight, and the great need is simply to put no obstacles in their way. For all, however, humanness means basically a capacity for social relatedness in terms healthy for the individual child; a preoccupation with the individualistic can defeat the human potential just as fully as can the oversocialization which denies individuality its place.

The Child and the Future

Coming to our third and last major theme, the children of today as the progenitors of the people of future centuries, we can admit our ignorance of genetics and of cultural evolution and still see that the decisions we make in this era will start twigs bending in one direction rather than another, and that the personal mental health and well-being as well as the wise decisions of today's children will in considerable measure guide the generations and centuries which follow in achieving sounder and sounder decisions about human living. Decisions impetuously made today to correct or overcorrect the mistakes of yesterday are not necessarily the decisions which are the best guide to very long-range living in the culture which is to be. In the long, long range the answer is always to get more evidence through science and through exploration, through the arts and new modes of social living, rather than through dogmatic standardization.

EXCELLENCE AND EQUALITY

by JOHN W. GARDNER

WILLIAM JAMES once said, "Democracy is on trial, and no one knows how it will stand the ordeal. . . . What its critics now affirm is that its preferences are inveterately for the inferior. Mediocrity enthroned and institutionalized, elbowing everything superior from the highway, this, they tell us, is our irremediable destiny."

William James was quoting the critics of democracy. He himself did not believe that mediocrity was our destiny. And I do not think that most people today believe it. Certainly I do not. But we would be very foolish indeed if we ignored the danger.

One might suppose that nothing could be less controversial than the relative merits of mediocrity and excellence. Yet people who set out to promote excellence often find that they have got themselves into a slugging match they cannot possibly win. The truth is that when it comes to the pursuit of excellence, there are some ways of going about it which Americans will accept and some ways which are offensive to them. Anyone who believes—as I do—that the en-

John W. Gardner is President of the Carnegie Corporation of New York.

couragement of excellence is about as important a goal as Americans could have today had better understand the hazards that line the course—and how to get around them. If anyone thinks that I am exaggerating the difficulties and wants to test this, let him launch a really vigorous campaign to promote excellence in his local school system—and see what happens.

In the first place, he will discover that there are people in the community who have very little fondness for democracy, and who never did believe in the widespread extension of educational opportunity. They will welcome his remarks in favor of excellence as an attack on democratic concepts of education and will promptly offer to join in on an attack on the school system. If he accumulates allies of that sort, his usefulness in the community will be at an end.

On the other side he will discover that there are some people in the community who believe that any reference to excellence is an attack upon American ideals of equality, and will accuse him of trying to create an elite.

At this point he will seriously consider going back to stamp-collecting, or bridge, or whatever that peaceful hobby was that he indulged in before becoming interesting in the schools. Unless one knows precisely what one believes in and what is meant by excellence, one is going to have a difficult time of it. But there is no greater service that can be done for a community than to help it to think clearly about these issues.

There are a good many Americans who have a genuine desire for excellence but have never really been clear in their own minds as to whether this was at odds with American ideals of equality. This is a question with which we had better deal head-on. What do we mean by equality? Do we mean any more or less than the Irishman when he said, "I'm as good as you are, and a great deal better, too"? Let us see what we do mean.

The eighteenth-century philosophers who made *equality* a central term in our political vocabulary never meant to imply that men are equal in all respects, in all dimensions, in all attributes of their persons and their lives. Nor do Americans today take such a view. It is possible to state in fairly simple terms the views concerning equality that would receive most widespread endorsement in our country today. The most fundamental of these views is simply that in the final matters of human existence all men are equally worthy of our care and concern. Further, we believe that men should be equal in the enjoyment of certain familiar legal, civil, and political rights. They should be, as the phrase goes, equal before the law.

But men are unequal in their native capacities and in their motivations, and therefore in their attainments. The most widely accepted means of dealing with this problem has been to emphasize *equality of opportunity*. The great advantage of the conception of equality of opportunity is that it candidly recognizes differences in native capacity and in willingness to work and accepts the certainty of differences in achievement. By allowing free play to these differences it preserves the freedom to excel, which counts for so much in terms of individual aspiration and has produced so much of mankind's greatness.

At the same time one must admit that the conception of equality has its limitations and ambiguities. In practice it means an equal chance to compete within the framework of rules established by the society in question; and this framework tends to favor certain kinds of people with certain kinds of gifts. This is unavoidable, but it is only proper that it be recognized. We must also recognize that in a society in which there are substantial differences from one family to another in wealth, learning, and concern for education, the formal equality of opportunity represented by free schooling may never erase the tremendous variations in opportunity represented by home background. In other words, we cannot assume that we have put our perplexities behind us when we assert our devotion to equality of opportunity.

So much for the conceptions of equality which would win almost universal acceptance in the United States today. But a good many Americans have gone considerably further in their equalitarian views. They have believed that no man should be regarded as better than another in any dimension.

People holding this view have tended to believe, for example, that men of great leadership capacities, great energies, or greatly superior aptitudes are more trouble to society than they are worth. Merle Curti reminds us that in the Jacksonian era in this country, equalitarianism reached such heights that trained personnel in the public service were considered unnecessary. "The democratic faith further held that no special group might mediate between the common man and the truth, even though trained competence might make the difference between life and death." Thus in the West, even licensing of physicians was lax, because not to be lax was thought to be undemocratic.

In such efforts to force a spurious equality, we can detect not only the hand of the generous man who honestly regrets that some must lose the foot race, but the hand of the envious man who resents achievement, who detests superiority in others, who will punish eminence at every opportunity.

Whether through the efforts of generous men or envious men, we have seen enough of this extreme equalitarianism to know what it implies. We have seen mediocrity breed mediocrity. We have seen the tyranny of the least common denominator.

In short, we now understand what Kierkegaard meant when he warned us of the danger of an equalitarianism so extreme as to be "unrelieved by even the smallest eminence." We now know what Flexner meant when he said, "We have to defend the country against mediocrity, mediocrity of souls, mediocrity of ideas, mediocrity of action. We must also fight against it in ourselves."

It is understandable that Americans should be cautious about excessive emphasis upon the difference in native capacity between one individual and another. Enemies of democracy have often cited the unequal capacities of men as justification for political and social philosophies which violate our most deeply held beliefs.

But we cannot escape the fact of individual differences

and we cannot escape the necessity of coping with them. Whether we like it or not, they are a central fact in any educational system—and indeed in any society. The good society is not one that ignores them but one that deals with them wisely and compassionately. This is the nub of the problem of excellence in a free society. It is the problem of dealing wisely and constructively with individual differences.

In education, for example, if we ignore individual differences we end up treating everyone alike—and one result is that we do not demand enough of our ablest youngsters. That is precisely the error we have made in recent decades. But if we toughen up the program and still ignore individual differences we only do an injustice to the average youngster who will have to drop by the wayside. The only solution is to admit that individuals differ and provide different treatment for different levels of ability. And never forget that we must do a good job at every level of ability. Our kind of society calls for the maximum development of individual potentialities at all levels.

But how does one provide different treatment for different levels of ability? That is where the arguments begin. Should we allow bright youngsters to skip grades, or should we observe the lockstep in which no one advances faster than anyone else? Should we have separate schools for the gifted as Admiral Rickover recommends, or comprehensive high schools as James B. Conant recommends?

I am not going to suggest specific solutions. I am going to lay down some principles to keep in mind if anything intelligent is to be done about this problem.

The first thing we must recognize if we are to deal wisely

with individual differences is that Americans are extremely
reluctant to put labels on differences in general capacity.
This is a deeply rooted national characteristic and anyone
who ignores it does so at his peril. We do not like any ar-
rangement which seems to suggest that some youngsters in
our schools are first-class citizens and others second-class citizens.

An example of this is to be found in the broad interpretation which we give to the phrase "college education." When
youngsters are graduated from high school we discuss those
going on to college as though they were a homogeneous lot,
all headed for a similar experience. Actually, a behind-the-
scenes view of the process will reveal that they are quietly
but fairly effectively sorted out.

At the key point in the sorting process is the high-school
dean. The students need not listen to his advice but usually
do. He sends his college-bound students out along widely
diverging pathways—to colleges of the highest possible standards, to colleges of moderate difficulty, and so on down to
colleges which may actually be lower academically than the
high school from which the youngster is being graduated.
But although the essence of his job is to arrive at clear appraisals of the relative standings of colleges and the relative
capacities of students, the high-school dean will ordinarily
take considerable care not to make these appraisals explicit
in his talks with students and parents.

This reluctance makes some critics extremely impatient.
But this is a point on which the American people insist—and
for my part I am glad that they do.

One way of looking at this national reluctance to label in-

dividual differences is that it is nonsensical and that we have
developed a ridiculous squeamishness about such matters.
Critics trace it to our desire to make young people "happy,"
to our concern for psychological adjustment. But such critics
are barking up the wrong tree. The reason we are reluctant
to label individual differences in native capacity is that native
capacity holds a uniquely important place in our scheme of
things. It must never be forgotten that ours is one of the
relatively few societies in the history of the world in which
performance is a primary determinant of status. More than
in any other society, in the United States the individual's
standing is determined by his capacity to perform. In a stratified society—a class society—the individual's standing, his
status, is determined by his family, by the class into which
he was born. Performance is not an important factor in establishing the individual's status so he can afford to be less
deeply concerned about his native capacity. In our society the
individual's future depends to an unprecedented degree upon
his native gifts.

Of course, we are oversimplifying matters greatly in using
such general terms as "native capacity." There are all kinds
of native capacity. That is a point to which we shall return
later. But for complex reasons, Americans see appraisals of
"intelligence," however defined, as total judgments on the
individual and as central to his self-esteem.

Some critics note that we discriminate nicely between excellence and mediocrity in athletics, but refuse to be similarly
precise about differences in intelligence; and they attribute
this to the fact that we are more seriously concerned with

and excellent first-grade teachers. The whole tone and fiber of our society depends upon a pervasive and almost universal striving for good performance.

And you are not going to have that kind of morale, that kind of striving, that kind of alert and proud attention to performance unless you can sell the whole society on a conception of excellence that leaves room for everybody who is willing to strive for it—a conception of excellence which means that whoever I am or whatever I am doing, if I am engaged in a socially acceptable activity, some kind of excellence is within my reach.

Those, then, are the three principles which I consider basic for dealing constructively with individual differences in education: First, to avoid arrangements which unnecessarily diminish the dignity of the less able youngster; second, to preserve the principle of multiple chances; and third, to recognize the many kinds and levels of excellence which we need and must nourish in a healthy society.

In applying these principles to the school system, the important thing is to keep the fundamental goal in mind: to deal wisely and constructively with individual differences, not to ignore them, not to brush them aside, not to pretend that they do not exist.

And when you have got yourself into a position to deal with each youngster in terms of his own potentialities and his own level of competence, then you can justly require that every youngster be *stretched* in terms of his own capacities; he must be expected to strive to the limit of performance of which he is capable. All high performance takes place with a framework of expectations, especially where young people are concerned. No expectations, no performance. We need not—indeed we must not—expect all of our youngsters to reach the same standard of performance. But we must expect that every youngster will strive to achieve the best that *he* is capable of achieving. If we do not expect it we are certain not to get it.

As to the down-to-earth practical arrangements which make it possible to deal with each youngster in terms of his ability, there are great differences of opinion among teachers. Many favor a certain amount of acceleration, that is, grade skipping, but others are opposed to it. Most educators now accept the need for grouping by ability, that is, putting youngsters of the same level of aptitude into the same class-room, but again, others are opposed to this. I happen to favor the system recommended by James Conant—a system called *sectioning by subject matter*. In this system the youngster might be in the advanced section in mathematics, but not in history. And youngsters of all levels of ability attend the same school and join in the same school activities. There are no distinctions between them outside the classroom.

But it is important not to be an inflexible advocate of any one system. Flexibility is the rule. The important thing is to keep the objective in mind. The means should be fitted to the situation, and in some cases to the individual. It may be that acceleration will be useful in some cases, but injurious in others. It may be that in some schools, one kind of group-ing by ability is natural and workable and in other schools another kind is workable.

In some big cities, special high schools for unusually gifted youngsters have proven effective. It is foolish to be dogmatic about these matters. The important thing is to find solutions somehow.

What we want is a system in which youngsters at every level of ability are stretched to their best performance and get the maximum education of which they are capable. We do not want any youngster to feel that he is unworthy or lacking in human dignity because of limitations in aptitude, but we do want to see our ablest youngsters encouraged, stimulated, and inspired to reach the heights of performance of which they are capable. I like to think that we are now sufficiently mature as a people to keep both of those objectives in mind and not to slight either of them.

SUGGESTED READING

THE GENETIC POTENTIAL by JAMES V. NEEL, M.D.

Goodman, H. C. and C. N. Herndon. "Genetic Factors in the Etiology of Mental Retardation," *International Records of Medicine* (1959), vol. 172.

National Academy of Sciences: National Research Council. *The Biological Effects of Radiation*. Washington, D.C., 1956.

Neel, James V. and W. J. Schull. *Human Heredity*. Chicago, University of Chicago Press, 1954.

Penrose, L. S. *The Biology of Mental Defect*. New York, Grune and Stratton, 1949.

Scheinfeld, A. *The New You and Heredity*. Philadelphia, Lippincott, 1950.

Stern, C. *Principles of Human Genetics*. San Francisco, Freeman, 1949.

GROWTH AND DEVELOPMENT by STANLEY M. GARN

Garn, Stanley M. and Z. Shamir. *Methods for Research in Human Growth*. Springfield, Ill., Thomas, 1958.

Mintz, Beatrice, ed. *Environmental Influences on Prenatal Development*. Chicago, University of Chicago Press, 1958.

Tanner, J. M. *Growth at Adolescence*. Oxford, Oxford University Press, 1955; Springfield, Ill., Thomas, 1955.

Zubek, J. P. and P. A. Solberg. *Human Development*. New York, McGraw-Hill, 1954.

THE DEVELOPMENT OF BEHAVIOR AND PERSONALITY by JOHN E. ANDERSON

Anderson, John E. *The Psychology of Development and Personality Adjustment.* New York, Holt, 1949.

Blair, A. W. and W. H. Burton. *Growth and Development of the Preadolescent.* New York, Appleton Century Crofts, 1951.

Erikson, E. H. *Childhood and Society.* New York, Norton, 1953.

Havighurst, Robert J. *Human Development and Education.* New York, Longmans Green, 1953.

Stone, L. J. and J. Church. *Childhood and Adolescence.* New York, Random House, 1957.

EDUCATIONAL OBJECTIVES OF AMERICAN DEMOCRACY by RALPH W. TYLER

Alcorn, Marvin D. and James M. Linley, eds. *Issues in Curriculum Development.* Yonkers, World, 1959.

Chase, Francis S. and Harold A. Anderson, eds. *The High School in a New Era.* Chicago, University of Chicago Press, 1958.

Henry, Nelson B., ed. *Adapting Secondary Schools to the Needs of Youth.* National Society for the Study of Education, 52d Yearbook, Part I. Chicago, University of Chicago Press, 1953.

Hunnicutt, Clarence W., ed. *Education 2000 A.D.* Syracuse, University of Syracuse Press, 1956.

WASTED TALENT by HORACE MANN BOND

Bond, Horace Mann. *The Search for Talent.* Cambridge, Harvard University Press, 1959.

French, Joseph L., ed. *Educating the Gifted.* New York, Holt, 1959.

Ginzberg, Eli. *The Negro Potential.* New York, Columbia University Press, 1956.

Wechsler, D. *Range of Human Capacities.* Revised ed. Baltimore, Williams and Wilkins, 1952.

Wolfle, Dale. *America's Resources of Specialized Talent.* New York, Harper, 1954.

THE ARMED FORCES AS A TRAINING INSTITUTION
by HAROLD WOOL

Ginzberg, Eli et al. *The Ineffective Soldier.* 3 vols. Vol. 3, *Patterns of Performance.* New York, Columbia University Press, 1959.

National Manpower Council. *A Policy for Skilled Manpower.* New York, Columbia University Press, 1954.

President's Commission on Veterans' Pensions. *Veterans' Benefits in the United States.* 3 vols. Washington, D.C., Government Printing Office, 1956.

Thorndike, Robert L. and Elizabeth P. Hagen. *Attitudes, Educational Programs, and Job Experiences of Airmen Who Did Not Reenlist.* Air Force Personnel and Training Research Center, 1957.

U.S. Department of the Air Force. *United States Air Force Occupational Handbook, 1959-60.* Washington, D.C., Government Printing Office.

U.S. Department of the Army. *Army Occupations and You.* Revised edition. Washington, D.C., Government Printing Office, 1956.

U.S. Department of Defense. *The Military Service Outlook.* Washington, D.C., Government Printing Office, 1959.

————. Defense Advisory Committee on Professional and Technical Compensation. *A Modern Concept of Manpower Management and Compensation for Personnel of the Uniformed Services.* Vol. 2. Washington, D.C., Government Printing Office, 1957.

U.S. Department of the Navy. *United States Navy Occupational Handbook, 1959.* Washington, D.C., Government Printing Office.

U.S. Marine Corps. *A Guide to Occupational Training.* Revised ed. Washington, D.C., Government Printing Office, 1959.

RELIGION AND YOUTH by BENSON Y. LANDIS

Allport, Gordon W. *The Individual and His Religion.* New York, Macmillan, 1950.
Argyle, Michael. *Religious Behavior.* Glencoe, Ill., Free Press, 1959.
Aronson, Sidney. *Religious Revival and Jewish Family Life.* New York, Synagogue Council of America, 1957. Mimeographed.
Fichter, Joseph H. *Sociology.* Chicago, University of Chicago Press, 1957.
Hollingshead, A. B. *Elmtown's Youth.* New York, Wiley, 1949.
Rettig, Solomon and Benjamin Pasamanick. "Changes in Moral Values Over Three Decades," *Social Problems,* VI (Spring, 1959).
Ross, Murray G. *Religious Beliefs of Youth.* New York, Association Press, 1950.

THE CHILD AS POTENTIAL by GARDNER MURPHY *and* LOIS BARCLAY MURPHY

American Council on Education, Commission on Teacher Education. *Helping Teachers Understand Children.* New York, 1945.
Del Castillo, Michel. *Child of Our Time.* New York, Knopf, 1958.
Murphy, Gardner. *Human Potentialities.* New York, Basic Books, 1958.
Murphy, Lois Barclay. *Able to Cope.* New York, Basic Books, 1960.
———. *Colin: A Normal Child.* New York, Basic Books, 1956.
Stone, L. J. and J. Church. *Childhood and Adolescence.* New York, Random House, 1957.